WORKER
IN THE
LIGHT

WORKER
IN THE
LIGHT

Unlock Your Five Senses and Liberate
Your Limitless Potential

GEORGE NOORY
AND
WILLIAM J. BIRNES

A TOM DOHERTY ASSOCIATES BOOK
NEW YORK

A Forge Book
Published by Tom Doherty Associates, LLC
175 Fifth Avenue
New York, NY 10010

www.tor.com

Forge® is a registered trademark of Tom Doherty Associates, LLC.

Book design by Mary A. Wirth

ISBN-13: 978-0-765-31087-3
ISBN-10: 0-765-31087-2

First Edition: September 2006

Printed in the United States of America

0 9 8 7 6 5 4 3 2 1

A Note to Our Readers

This is a book in which we present alternate realities and ways to gather information within those realities. In many cases, we report on the views of guests on *Coast to Coast AM* and of other researchers and writers. Those views are not necessarily our views and we report them for information only. We do not offer medical advice or opinions. Readers should consult their own health care professionals regarding medical issues. With respect to the diet information and the psychic exercises set forth in this book, we caution readers that these are for information only and advise readers to proceed at their own risk and with due care.

Please also be advised that some of the names of individuals and details of the events we describe have been changed or deleted.

GEORGE NOORY AND WILLIAM J. BIRNES

I dedicate *Worker in the Light* to my loving mother, Georgette, who showed me the light many years ago when she gave me the book *We Are Not Alone.*

GEORGE NOORY

To my late parents, Abe Kaplan and Vi Katz, who worked on *The Jack Benny Program* and *Burns and Allen* on radio and had their own radio act when radio was what the Internet is today, I dedicate this book, in memory of "Burns and Kaye." And to the future: This is for Casey Birnes Grindle.

WILLIAM J. BIRNES

CONTENTS

ACKNOWLEDGMENTS

To our publisher at Tor/Forge, Tom Doherty; our editors, Robert Gleason and Eric Raab; and my literary agents, David Vigliano and Celeste Fine of Vigliano Associates. To Marina Aluisa for her inspiration, and my children, Wendy, Kristina, and Jonathan, for putting up with me. To my producer, Lisa Lyon, who never ceases to amaze me. To Alan Corbeth and Art Bell for the "opportunity of a lifetime." To Kraig Kitchin, my network president and a man of tremendous character; Ron Barber, a man of great insight; and my father, Gabriel, whom I will love until the end of time and beyond.

GEORGE NOORY

To Nancy Hayfield Birnes, my wife and the inspiration for every good thing I do, particularly working in the light, and to our editors and publisher at Tor/Forge. I want to acknowledge the groundbreaking work of Dr. Harold Puthoff, Ingo Swann, Paul H. Smith, the early developers of coordinate remote viewing, and all the pioneers who dared challenge conventional wisdom and pushed the envelope of human knowledge and awareness. This book celebrates their work.

WILLIAM J. BIRNES

INTRODUCTION

by George Noory

We rational human beings think of our lives as bounded by our five palpable senses. But what if someone were to prove to you conclusively that we have more senses at our disposal than anyone could ever imagine? What if someone demonstrated to you with a scientific accuracy that you yourself have sensory abilities that allow you to navigate through time and space without a machine and even to see into your future? No, it's not magic. It's not even supernatural. It's as natural as touching a surface and sensing whether you're touching metal or the bark of a tree. This discovery of another sense was an experience I had when I was eleven or twelve and, during a bout with a fever, I discovered that I had the ability to levitate out of my body and float to the ceiling. What a discovery that was. Since then I have researched the realm of "higher sensory ability." I have made attaining an understanding of this form of perception one of my life's goals.

A very select group of people has known about our innate

higher sensory abilities and has handed down this knowledge to successive generations for thousands of years. Indigenous peoples around the world have taught the skills of higher sensory perception. And today, scientists at more than a few universities have demonstrated that a higher sensory perceptivity exists, is quantifiable, and can be reproduced under laboratory x conditions. In fact, even our own military and intelligence agencies have used higher sensory perceptivity not only to spy on our enemies, but to travel across the solar system, and even travel in time.

What they know, I want you to know. In the following pages, I will reveal the secrets of higher sensory perceptivity, remote viewing, intuition management, out-of-body projection, and even time travel. I want you to know how to be a worker in the matrix, a worker in the light of the multiverse, a thoroughly empowered human being using all of your senses to connect with the great link of all creation. *Worker in the Light* is a book about human empowerment, spiritual enlightenment, ultimate productivity, and absolute happiness. It's a gift of the ages, a gift of such self-empowerment that just knowing you are capable of it is enough to change your life forever. And this gift is yours to keep.

Come with me on a journey that will show you powers you never dreamed you had and show you how to work and live in the light.

WORKER
IN THE
LIGHT

CHAPTER

1

THE OUIJA BOARD

It came in an old nondescript box addressed to me.

A fan had sent it.

With a simple, "Here," a studio technician handed me the box just before I went on the air.

I had no idea what it was. Maybe it was a gift given in good conscience. Maybe someone sent it to me on a dare. I'll never know for sure. Whatever the sender's intention, the weathered and worn Ouija board inside the box ultimately took me to the very edge of reality, from which point I looked over the brink into an unfathomable black pool of chaos.

Why is it that such an innocuous piece of cardboard with its triangular-shaped planchette holds the threat of becoming a force for evil? This was not a question that came to mind that late-night in the KTRS studios in St. Louis as I was hosting *Coast to Coast AM* back in 2002, filling in for the legendary Art Bell.

I was taking calls, as usual, from listeners who had experienced their own encounters with the paranormal: ghosts of loved ones, voices offering help or consolation from the other side, cats or dogs whose behavior mysteriously foretold of danger, shadow people you could see just out of the corner of your eye, Big Foot, the giant bird, Mothman, UFOs of all shapes and sizes, and flying triangles. People were calling on open lines about abductions and other traumatic events that had shaped their lives. And then I told my audience about the

Ouija board in the antique box. Should I use it on the air, I asked the listeners?

Calls came pouring in, jamming the switchboard, the first-time caller line, and all the wildcard lines: "Do it!"

I slid the Ouija board out of its box.

Now, for anyone who has never seen the inside of a modern radio broadcast studio, the sight of so many switches, dials, flashing indicator lights, and phone hookups, all set around a table festooned with standing and hanging microphones and computer monitors for reading e-mail can be intimidating. On those very few occasions when I have hosted in-studio guests, I always tried to let them get acclimated to the array of equipment well before we went on the air so that there'd be no dead time between questions and answers in an interview because the overwhelming presence of technology had distracted a guest's attention.

This amount of technology is comforting to me, because I know I'm hardwired into the rest of the universe. However, for every diode, switch, and electronic circuit there are probably a hundred things that will cause them to fail. That's why you have redundant and back-up systems and why you have a studio engineer as well as a producer backing you up and reading the dials to make sure the system's working the way it's supposed to. It's complicated, but it's only electronics. It's science.

For every equipment failure, there's a physical reason. And for every failure there's a fix. That's what you learn on the job. That's what your engineer signals to you when a piece of equipment goes dead and you stare blankly through a glass window at the producer. That's what you have to rely on when nothing is coming through your earphones.

On this particular night in St. Louis, amid the mass of

electronics and blinking lights arrayed all around me like a nice warm security envelope, I unfolded the Ouija board and set it on the studio desk. I felt a hesitation. Should I or shouldn't I? The listener calls kept flooding in. Voices in my earphones were egging me on in front of a ten-million-person audience stretched almost 5,000 miles diagonally across the entire continent from Halifax in Canada to National City, California, on the Mexican border.

"Hi, George, this is Josh from Watertown. Ask it a question."

But I remembered *The Exorcist*, as well as countless other movies, when the person about to become the innocent victim finds that the pointer is out of his or her control and the demonic voice speaks through that person's fingertips. Sure I hesitated. Who wouldn't?

My audience was insistent.

"I have a question, George."

"Can it talk to the dead?"

A truck driver phoned in from somewhere along an interstate outside of Lawrence, Kansas. He, too, had a question begging for an answer.

I took the planchette out of the box.

Okay, I thought, maybe just once. I told the audience what I was doing, placing my fingertips lightly on the planchette so as to let whatever force was present guide the reader across the letters laid out along the board. Ask a yes or no question, the planchette will direct you. Ask for a name or a word, and the planchette will spell it out. Remember every B horror film you've ever seen where the camera does a close focus on a pair of hands being guided by something out of their control, and you'll know exactly what I'm talking about.

"Okay," I said to the audience. "I'm ready. Call in with a question and let's see what this baby can do. The numbers again are . . ."

Darkness, sudden and terrifying. Not even the diodes were blinking.

Before my eyes could adjust, the lights came on again. The back-up generators had kicked in and the studio came alive.

"What was that?" I heard one of the engineers say through my earphones.

"You're supposed to know," another voice said. Maybe it was my in-studio producer, Howard Morton. "Are we on generators?"

There was a lot of background chatter as I stared down at the planchette on the Ouija board. It was pointing to "No."

"Hey, George, I got a question," a caller's voice crackled through the earphones. He was on a cell phone, I could tell.

"Go ahead," I said. But just then my earphones went dead.

I signaled to my producer on the other side of the thick glass window that separated the control room from the broadcast booth, "Are we on?"

He gave me a thumbs-up back, but I still couldn't hear anything coming out of the earphones. I pointed to my ear and gave him the cut sign across my neck. Audio was dead to me. I could see him check his board and shake his head. Then the sound came back.

"So what do you think, George? Can you ask it?" The caller's voice said.

"Hey, my friend, you broke up out there," I said, hoping that it was his phone and not our audio. "Run that by me again?"

I looked down. The planchette was still sitting on "No,"

only this time it seemed as if it had moved a little. My hands were resting on it, but I felt nothing.

My caller began speaking when, as suddenly as the lights had gone out moments earlier, all the dials on the panels in front of me dropped to zero as if somebody had pulled the plug. I still had sound in my earphones, but none of the instruments were registering. And, again, I shot a what's up look to my producer, who only shrugged and then gave me a thumbs-up.

"We're having some difficulty here with the line," I said to my caller, who, by now, was getting impatient. "So I thank you for dialing in." And I cut off the call.

"Why?" I could lipread my producer through the glass.

I shrugged again. I didn't know. It was as if some poltergeist were playing tricks with the equipment. But I went back to the Ouija board as another call came in with a question, this one really spooky, about, "Who was the spirit attending to the board?"

"What do you mean?" I asked the caller.

"The boards have spirits sometimes," the caller said, assuring the audience that she had used Ouija boards many times and had communicated with spirits speaking through them and guiding the planchette over the letters. "You can ask it a question and it will identify itself."

My producer's attention was riveted on the caller as she explained that I had to concentrate my full attention on the board and ask the board to spell out the name of the spirit.

As I began to focus, the entire studio went black again and, this time, even the computers lost power. I could hear a multitude of voices in my earphones, lots of yelling, and the frantic sounds of engineers shouting to technicians. Then the auxiliary generators kicked in, the lights came up, dimmed, and then went out again. The studio was dead.

Next thing I knew, amid the darkness that seemed blacker than a moonless night, the door from the control room burst open with a crash and in flew Howard Morton, my producer.

"Give me that damn thing," he said, without even telling me what he meant. But I sensed it anyway.

He took the Ouija board out of my hands, stuffed it back in the box, threw the planchette in after it, and folded the flaps closed.

"Now I'm getting this thing out of here."

And he tossed it through the control room door to another technician.

The lights came up. I could hear the hum of the generators' winding motors, and suddenly the dials on the panels in front of me shot up to their nominal levels. Diodes and LEDs began to flicker, and I heard the soft sound of the computer hard drive heads engage. We were back.

"You know what, caller from Texas," I said into the mike. "We just got rid of the Ouija board. It was the darndest thing you ever saw."

"I copy that," the caller said. "I was gonna warn you about it but you beat me to it." And with a click the caller was gone into the vast great link of people who comprise the *Coast to Coast* audience, invisible except for their presence over the phone.

The rest of the show, all three and a half hours of it, proceeded as if nothing had happened. It was normal—if you can call my shows normal—as any other night with callers talking about ghosts, aliens, creatures like Big Foot, and other paranormal encounters. Truckers phoned in from the road about mystery truck stops that served home-cooked meals at 1950s prices with real homemade mashed red-skin potatoes and then couldn't be found again on that same stretch of highway when the truckers went back to look for them. And other people talked about angels. My guest that night talked about the ancient pyramids and the theories of the Sphinx, and my producer performed as he did on every other night. And at four in the morning when we signed off, he handed me the Ouija board in its box and told me, in very specific terms, to keep it out of our studio. He never wanted to see the thing again. And I told him that's exactly what I would do.

It was close to five in the morning by the time I got back to the house, and even though it was still dark in St. Louis, I could hear the first trills of birds in the trees near the house. Early traffic—food trucks, and newspaper delivery vans—was already on the street. But for me it was time to go to bed.

Doing a late-night talk show is just like working a night shift. You're going to bed as the world is waking up. And St. Louis, like Detroit, Chicago, and other industrial cities, is a town of early risers. So, if you have to catch your requisite sleep to be sharp for the next night's show, you have to learn to sleep through the noise of trucks backing up outside your house, car horns blaring because someone was too slow to jump through a light that's just changed to green, and the crack-of-dawn trash pickup that clatters garbage can lids across the pavement.

This was a skill, sleeping through a cacophony of morning noise, that I had honed over the years as the St. Louis "Nighthawk." But this morning, with the Ouija board still on the backseat of my car, every little sound got me up. I turned over, pulled the covers up over my ears, told myself to go back to sleep. But at the next sound I was up again, noticing through the window that the sun was edging up to its 9 A.M. position. This was going to be more frustrating than it was worth. So I got up, cleaned up, and headed down to the KTRS studio. They had the best tea in town, anyway.

I had a disquieting feeling that I couldn't shake off, a feeling that I had peeked over the edge of normal reality into another world. I had a sense that there were things out there, bad things, that were bouncing against the closed door of our reality, looking for a way to slip through a crack. It was the Ouija board, I was sure of it, that had become a crack. Had I let something in last night? Had the individual who sent me the board in the old box tempted me with a Trojan Horse to bring something potentially lethal into this world? And had something escaped, which was now linked to me?

Then my rational voice took over. Ouija boards had been around for over a century. And this one was just a piece of cardboard. Look at the box. It had a manufacturer's trademark on it. It was printed somewhere in Illinois, not in Styx or in Hades. It was a Ouija board, nothing more. But it brought back memories of other times I'd looked over the edge of the world into an abyss of mystery, like the time I first realized there was another reality.

I was eleven or twelve when it happened.

I think I must have had a fever at the time. But all I remember is that I felt very tired and was on the verge of sleep. I felt my body vibrate strangely and I couldn't move any of my muscles. Then when I opened my eyes, I was on the ceiling looking down at myself.

I had no feeling of levitation. No sense that I was moving. No sense of the passage of time. One second I was lying in my own bed, I felt a shaking, and the next second I was looking down. There I was, in two places at once. I was on the ceiling and there I was on the bed, a little kid with a face like the comedian Buddy Hackett.

"This must be a dream," I told myself as I saw myself on the bed below. But it felt like no dream I'd ever had. And even now, remembering it, I cannot call it a dream.

But human beings do not normally float in air except in dreams. So when the realization struck that I was actually outside my body looking down, in an instant, I found myself back down in my own body and was looking up at the ceiling again. There was no sense of movement and no feeling that I had awakened from sleep. I was one place, then I was in another. Life had returned to normal, or so it seemed.

It would have been easy to have written this off as a dream or a kind of hallucinatory state between waking and dreaming brought on by either a fever or just plain fatigue. And for a few seconds after I realized what had happened, that's just what I tried to do: deny it had happened. Call it a dream and pack it up. But I couldn't shelve it that easily, and it has stayed in my memory ever since just like a warning light, telling me that there was something beyond the four walls, an existence outside of one's own body, a piece of personal evidence that human beings can float in the air, can fly, can look down at their own three-dimensional bodies and acknowledge that there is another state of being.

At that moment I was not bound by the limitations of gravity because I was on the ceiling looking down. I was not bound by the physical limitations of my own body because I was outside of it, looking at it. I was not even bound by the limitations of time because I seemed to be outside of it as well.

It was only when I was aware that I was looking down that I floated back into my body. Maybe those old *Road Runner* cartoons had it right when Wiley Coyote runs over the cliff, stays poised mid air, then looks down and plummets to earth. This ultimately became a life-changing experience for me, an introduction to a reality in which what was supposed to be was not.

BORN FOR THIS JOB

Some people train for the jobs they have. Other people seem to be born for it. I believe that I was born for this job of hosting Coast to Coast, *but that I trained for it by learning so much about the paranormal and navigating myself through the world of intuition and remote viewing, thereby honing a skill I was blessed with as a child. I've always been interested in the paranormal. I've always believed that human beings have abilities to sense, or "extra sense," the emotions and thoughts of other people. Although I couldn't put this into words until I began speaking to my distant relative whom I called "Aunt Shafica" and learning from my guests on my Nighthawk program in St. Louis, I still believed that if I turned off my judgmental voice and simply listened and tried to sense the emotions of the person speaking to me, I would know a lot more than if I tried to be logical. You need logic in a job like mine, of course, because you have to be able to figure out what does and doesn't make sense to you. I learned to figure out when to turn the logic off and go by instinct and when to turn the logic back on. They're two different kinds of filters. Logic filters out my own emotions and my instinct filters out the logic. It's a balancing act, which, when you learn to do it, can make you a very powerful person.*

I do believe that it was my momentary out-of-body experience that launched me on the quest to find out about the other reality that I had experienced. And, the lure of the other reality was so tantalizing that decades later, when I was on the radio, I decided to try an experiment, one with the dark side that taught me a lesson I almost forgot when I opened the Ouija board box.

This exercise in the transmission of negative personal energy, what I call the "dark side," took place in St. Louis about a year and a half before I received the Ouija board from a fan. I can't say for sure what made me play games with forces far more powerful than I, but even though my intentions at first were noble, it turned into wanting something so badly that I was willing to gamble with my own health to get it. It was honor, I thought at first, which then became love for a very beautiful woman. But in the end it was really an infatuation that suckered me in. We're all human, you know.

The escapade began simply enough with a desire to protect a young woman from a group of lounge lizard vultures, all of whom were behaving very badly. But as I became more deeply involved, I became possessive. I became so attracted to this woman that my emotions turned me around until my means became my ends. And when I finally achieved what I was after, it brought me no pleasure, only an empty feeling of triumph that quickly faded.

It all started one night at a party when I first spotted a gorgeous woman surrounded by a bunch of guys. She was petite, blond, and very young. She was as bright as a candle in a darkened room, and around her like so many birds of prey were the typical guys that populate the outer fringes of the entertainment industry. I recognized some of them: ad guys, promo guys, a couple of nerdy types, and a few rock band hangers-on: people around the periphery of top-40 radio. They hung on her like a blanket. But this young woman was poised. She ate up the attention she was getting. And yet I thought she needed my protection because she couldn't possibly know what these guys wanted. At least that's what I believed. So I was St. George, these were the dragons, and she was the damsel in distress.

I moved in on the cluster of guys, chatted her up, and then became part of the queue of men around her. And as I stood there, volleying with the conversation and fending off other guys getting their two cents in. I became just one of the group. Couldn't she see that these were guys after only one thing and I was protecting her from them? My intentions were honorable. Theirs weren't.

I felt territorial at first, natural male hormones at work. Then I got possessive. I was her knight in shining armor. Then I got angry that the guys around her didn't back off. It wasn't a hot anger and my blood didn't boil. Worse, it was a cold anger, cold and calculating and revenge-seeking. And it was self-serving, too. I got her name that night and, of course, knew who the other guys were who were trying to score a few points with her. And then I settled in to figure out what to do about them. Maybe put a white circle like a halo around her so that she would be enveloped in my protection. But my emotions took over.

The idea I came up with, in good faith at first, but calculating and possessive at the end because I'd given in to anger, wasn't very smart. But it was very effective. And it's not something anyone should do on his or her own because—and I say this from firsthand experience—it is sure to backfire. I located myself in a darkened room where I settled into a thick-cushioned easy chair with a high back and nice padded arms. I closed my eyes and focused on each of the men I wanted out of my way. I repeated each one's name to myself as I saw his face in my mind. And then, with all of the power I could muster from the depths of my psyche, I sent out the most evil thoughts I could imagine, specifically aimed at the individual. And this was not just a one-time exercise. I repeated it each night, deliberately and with the full understanding of what I was doing.

I willed evil to befall each individual. I conjured up each face as I closed my eyes and sent the most negative thoughts I could directly to the person represented by his face. I'm not proud of this.

I told myself at the time it was only an experiment, an answer to a question: If I sent negative thoughts out, would I achieve my aim? Then this became a nightly ritual, and soon the results began to pay off. Some of the men lost their jobs, others incurred severe financial reverses, and still others began to suffer medical problems. And the more I heard stories of the success of my negative energy, the more it fed on itself. One of the individuals got himself into a bizarre traffic accident. Still another began to have back pain so severe that it laid him up for over a month without any doctor being able to treat it because the reason for the pain was undiscoverable.

And as for the young woman, I sent out thoughts to influence her as well, isolating her from friends and family in the hopes that she would turn to me. In part, what I tried to do was based on a story I heard from another sailor who told it to me when I was in the Navy years and years earlier. This sailor, on a night we were swapping stories, told of a friend of his in college whom I'll call "Doom" and who practiced dark rituals in his dormitory room. It was the kind of story I would have had on *Coast*.

Doom was a sad but foreboding character, not the kind of guy who could walk up to a girl and ask her out. He was so introverted that it was almost impossible to pry him out of his shell. He simply walked along the halls, made his way to class, head hung low, eyes on the ground, and interacted with no one. But that didn't mean he didn't have feelings, deep urges about the girls in his classes to whom he was too shy to speak. Every so often, this sailor told me, he would see Doom pick up his head and eyeball a real cutie as she floated by him. If she were animatedly talking amid a flotilla of boys, a look of evil would cross Doom's face. But on the surface he would do nothing. And woe to the girl who befriended him or innocently flirted with him. And that's the point of this story.

There was one young woman in a history class with Doom and my friend from the Navy who, because she was very outgoing and spoke to everyone, thought nothing of engaging Doom in conversations now and then. She was a popular girl, who dated lots of guys and was very visible on campus. And she was very pleasant to look at, my friend told me. Doom, he said, confided to him that he had a plan to win her affections, but it was not something he would talk about. And shortly thereafter, this young woman began showing up in class with bruises, black-and-blue marks, and, one day, a burn on her arm. Over the course of the next few weeks, she seemed less animated, more subdued, and even had a brooding demeanor about her. Her smile had vanished and she was no longer the outgoing creature who had been the center of attention at the beginning of the semester, as if she had been wearing a halo of gold. By Thanksgiving she looked as bleak as the winter landscape in central Ohio where my friend had gone to school.

She was seen once at a party with Doom, very unhappy and withdrawn, and not at all like the person she once had been. Doom, on the other hand, appeared happy, triumphant even, as if he were proud of some accomplishment. But they were only seen together one time, and soon the young woman had disappeared completely. My friend found out months later that she had left school, gone home to her parents, after having had a serious accident in a gymnastics class. In a very simple exercise on the low horse, an exercise she had performed countless times, it was as if she had lost concentration, fell, and broke her leg. Months later, in a moment of rare disclosure, my friend said, Doom told him that she had been his conquest, the object of his focus. He had performed incantations, Doom said, nightly rituals in which he broke her confidence by visualizing her having accidents and becoming demoralized. And when he perceived that his magic was working, he befriended her, asked her out, and took her to at least one campus party. When she had tried to break away because Doom was freaking her out, he turned up the wattage on the mental energy he was projecting and, he bragged, forced her to have an accident. That was the story my friend told me when we were in the Navy.

I believe it was this story that played through my mind as I focused my mental energy on the young woman whose affections I wanted to win. And for a time it worked. None of the men I perceived as competitors came around anymore. Most of them had faced such serious reverses in work or in finances that they were unable to compete. Others had simply disappeared. I was alone with her in a circle of ruin that I had created around her. The negative thoughts I had projected to destroy the competition and demoralize the young woman had worked. But now it was time for me to experience what I had done.

It had begun with a simple accident, spilling tea water from the pot onto my hand instead of into the cup. But it started a chain reaction of calamities that morning from spilling the coffee onto my clothing, all over the kitchen counter; to short-circuiting the pot in the sink when I forgot to unplug it; to winding up blowing a breaker and crashing a computer that was connected to the same line; to realizing I was late for an appointment because I had spent too much time cleaning up the mess; and for just missing a collision when I ran a stop sign because I wasn't paying attention to my driving. It was an expensive ticket.

These kinds of falling domino mornings don't just happen. There is no coincidence in the universe, only unseen causality. I know that now and should have known it then. But I was putting it all aside because I was enjoying the company of this woman. I was her guardian, I told myself, protecting her from a world of predators and feeling my oats. But I had fallen victim to my illusions and wasn't putting two and two together.

My morning calamities soon became regular occurrences, accidents on top of accidents. They were just nuisances at first: spilled drinks, broken glasses, a rotisserie chicken or two that somehow managed to walk off the kitchen counter and onto the floor. But soon I developed a backache that wouldn't go away. Aspirin didn't help. Sit-ups, which normally help because they work out sore muscles, didn't help either. It wasn't a debilitating pain, but it was persistent and annoying and forced me to think about the pain whenever I moved. Bed rest and therapy helped it and told me there was nothing medically wrong with me, but it caught my attention.

Then I caught a cold, or so I thought, that wouldn't go away. Aspirin, cold medicine, lots of fluids, more bed rest, and the largest bowls of chicken soup you ever saw didn't make it get better. A blood test told me there was no flu. There wasn't even supposed to be a cold. The doctor just shook his head with an "I dunno" expression and told me to go back to bed. I felt miserable.

The cold got better, but I suddenly became accident-prone, banging my head, my elbow, and my legs against things that seemed to leap out at me from wherever I went. I was extraspecially careful, but I still managed to get bruises one after the other. And that was the least of it. My mind, in those times between waking and sleep, was flooded with dark thoughts and anxieties. I was fearful about the smallest of concerns. Molehills, not even, became mountains as I became awash in dark visions of ominous futures and catastrophes too big to wear down to manageable sizes.

What was the source of this fear, these visions? Why was my mind a playing field for demons? Were these perceptions of reality or my own creations? And if creations, why was I indulging myself in these self-destructive thoughts? Yet, at the same time, I was persisting in sending negative thoughts toward the guys I believed stood between me and the young lady whose honor I was protecting. Stories came back to me about the catastrophes befalling them while I was struggling with the dark thoughts pinning me to my bed in the early morning when, in the midst of a self-created fantasy of my own future undoing, a reality crashed in like a brick falling in through a skylight. There was nothing in my feelings of defeat that was real. No demons were after me. No enemies were seeking my discomfiture. *I was the one creating this reality.* The dark thoughts were coming out of me. Could I be the source of all of this?

I examined my own behavior as if I were under my own microscope. *I* was the one sending out the dark thoughts to engulf others. Regardless of my motivations—honorable at the beginning, I told myself—my means had ultimately defeated my motivations. Embracing the dark in order to achieve the light, although it had seemed like a benevolent experiment at the time, had become completely malignant in its results, a lesson I saw at once in stark relief. And, I discovered, the simple act of sending waves of darkness to flood the minds and lives of others had a reverberating effect. They bounced back to flood your own life and mind. It was as if I were living the old Yiddish story of the Golem in which the protagonist invoked a monstrous creature to wreak vengeance on its enemies only to find that monster eventually turned its demonic wrath on the one who invoked it. My own Golem had turned its attentions on me.

What had I done?

What to do?

Out of the pit of my own misery, as William Ernest Henley wrote in "Invictus"—"Out of the night that covers me,/Black as the Pit from pole to pole"—I remembered something I was taught by my father one night when I was very, very young, looking into a darkened room. My dad simply struck a match and held it up. Whatever shadows lurked there within the darkness disappeared. He said, "One candle all by itself will dispel the darkness around you." He said, "The darkest night is defeated by the flicker of a single flame."

Light defeats darkness just as a solitary good deed will cre- ✗ ate an angel who will stand up for you at the end of days. I remembered this. So I wondered, would the dark thoughts I was sending to others and that were flooding back onto me evaporate if I bathed my objects in a white light? Just as I experimented with the dark side, would I be able to pull myself back out of this hole if I simply switched off the negativity and consciously and meticulously replaced every dark thought with a bright one? It's not as easy as it sounds because the dark thoughts had become a matter of habit, like a muscle you use over and over again. It would mean a kind of mental and spiritual retraining to bring unused muscles back into use. But because I was falling deeper and deeper into the pot of gloom and was experiencing so many real-world accidents, I was game for any amount of work. So I concentrated on the light just like I had concentrated on the darkness.

It was a process. I said to myself that if I engulfed the woman of my intentions and her admirers with a bubble of white, evanescent light, representative of my best thoughts, nothing would happen to anyone. I did exactly what I had done before, sat in a chair in a room with subdued light, closed my eyes, and focused. Soon, this evening ritual became a form ⋎ of yoga. And soon things began to change.

I noticed that within the ensuing days, I was becoming less clumsy in the kitchen. I moved slower and with more deliberation and, as a result, there was less crashing into things. I felt better. My persistent cold seemed to dry up. And, most important, the terrors that plagued me in the early morning hours disappeared. Clearly, the reverberations from the black thoughts I was sending out had stopped and had been replaced with positive thoughts. If you had told me in advance that there was such a direct and simultaneous correlation between projecting dark thoughts and dark consequences that befall you I would not have believed you even though, I realize, I remembered the inscription that fourteenth-century English knights wore on their sashes, "Honi soit qui mal y pense," or, loosely translated, "Evil comes to him who thinks evil."

There will be many, many people who believe in the power of thought and prayer, but would love to have some physical reality to attach it to. I knew my dark thoughts were working, but I didn't know why. It wasn't like gravity or anything like that. Wouldn't it have been great to know that there was an actual physical event taking place as a result of all of my mental projections, something measurable and definable as if it were on a scientist's workbench, an objective correlative that you could latch onto, hold up, or even photograph? Now I know that there is just such a manifestation, and were I to have seen it years ago, it would have terminated my projections in less than a heartbeat.

What I did not know then, but know now, is that the experiments of Japanese researcher Dr. Masaru Emoto just about prove that projected thoughts have a real-world physical manifestation. Dr. Emoto developed a photographic technique to capture the crystallization of water just as the water freezes. To test out whether emotions and projected feelings have any effect on water, he focused his intention on a sample of water as it was crystallizing and then photographed the result. He discovered, and you can see the photographs themselves in his book *The Hidden Messages in Water,* that prayer and good focused thoughts result in perfectly symmetrical harmonious crystalline structures. Dark and hateful thoughts result in ugly, chaotic structures. It's as clear as the difference between black and white.

Why is this important? Think about this: our bodies are made of water. Water covers three-quarters of the planet. Water is the universal solvent and is an element in most everything in existence. In other words, water is everywhere and in everything including ourselves. Therefore, how our emotions affect water is how our emotions affect us. Thoughts, good and bad, $\times$ have a physical presence in the universe, a materiality to them that can make us sick, make us well, make us feel at peace, and make us feel at war. Projecting hatred is not only a display of emotion, it has a physical effect and a bounce-back effect on the actual chemistry of your own body. It leaves an impression on the essential element of our own bodies. Thus prayer has an actual, measurable, physical shape. The more prayer there is in the world, the more harmony there is. The more hatred there is in the world, the more the physical nature of the elements themselves is disrupted. Read Dr. Emoto's book and see the photographs for yourself. It will certainly show why a hurricane coming ashore and heavy with rain can actually be affected by the combined prayers of millions of individuals who want to weaken it or divert it from populated areas.

Memories of my experiment with projecting dark thoughts percolated through my brain as I drove to the studio the morning after the Ouija board incident, a reminder of the near disaster that had occurred the night before. It was the second time I had gone to the very edge and looked over into the world of misery where those who allow themselves to be taken over will find themselves.

I pulled into my parking space at the studio. It was still very early for me, but there was activity all over the studio. FedEx and UPS trucks were all over the parking lot, at least two U.S. Mail trucks were unloading, and equipment was coming in and going out on dollies. I took the Ouija board box out of the car, tucked it under my arm, and brought it back into the studio. I half suspected that the whole place would go down as I crossed the threshold of the doorway, but no such thing happened.

I took the elevator up to the broadcast studios floor and went over to where John, our morning-man, was holding court at his phone bank, batting high-energy callers back into their cars as they challenged him on a whole range of social issues. John uses lots of humor, in a way that makes his callers laugh, and that's what's made him a popular morning host. He saw me outside the glass, pointed to his wristwatch, and pretended to faint from shock. I held up the Ouija board box and he waved me in. This was another experiment. I figured that if the bad stuff the other night was coming out of me, the board would have no effect on Gaglia.

"And guess who's here?" John said into his microphone. "It's George Noory, and he's brought me a present. A present for all of you, too."

He paused and took the box out of my hand.

"Hey George, you're up early, no UFOs last night?"

He laughed into the mike and opened the Ouija board box.

"Whoa, folks, you'll never guess what George Noory brought in. It's a Ouija board. Get your questions ready."

I waved my hand and moved toward the door.

"Looks like George is heading home, folks, so its just the thousands of us here in the studio this morning. Ask me anything, folks and my Ouija board will answer. Hi, caller, where are you from?"

I was walking down the hall when the lights went out. I just kept on walking, didn't even stop at the office, got into my car and drove out of the parking lot. The wooden gate was frozen in the open position. I was barely halfway down the road to our local breakfast mom and pop restaurant when my cell phone rang. It was a furious ring, too.

"You can take this back," Gaglia said without even announcing himself. "My producer took it right out of the studio."

"That's okay," I told him. "Just toss it in the dumpster." And I snapped the phone shut and contemplated a buttermilk pancake breakfast.

CHAPTER

2

THE BACKGROUNDS
OF REMOTE VIEWING

I't's Christmas Eve in L.A.

I work the Christmas Eve show, just as I do all the major holidays. I host open lines. I'm there for folks to talk to on Christmas Eve after the kids have gone to bed and mom and dad are putting presents under the tree or for all those people who are working at jobs, behind the wheel of police cars on icy roads in Anytown, USA, driving trucks across desolate interstates at one in the morning, sitting at a security guard desk at a building in downtown Newark, stocking shelves at a Krogers in a shopping center outside of Dayton, an Albertson's in Roswell, or a D'Agostino's in Manhattan. I'm there for them.

Outside my studio, a winter rain has begun to fall. It starts out very light at first, just like a cloud coming in for a landing over the San Fernando Valley. Then as the evening wears on, it becomes a steady saturating rain amid the low-hanging clouds that obscure the bright lights along Ventura Boulevard. But it's snug and warm inside the studio, alive with analog dials and digital readouts. I'm at my horseshoe table, with seats for in-studio guests or for team hosts during the daytime broadcasts. But I'm alone at the mike tonight. My engineers are in the studio room, my studio producer, Tom, working the phones tonight.

The equipment runs 24-7 here at Premiere Radio—phone screen banks on computer screens, the many digital phone lines assigned to different numbers, and the intercom system that allows everyone to communicate. But at the start of each show, we make sure that everything is in working order anyway, just in case we have to make last-minute changes. Tom tells me everything checks out, I get a thumbs-up, my engineer starts counting down from ten to one, holding his hand right up in the air for the final five, then the bumper music comes up, the "live" light comes on, and we're live on *Coast to Coast AM* on Christmas Eve.

Over the years I've developed a loyal listening audience on Christmas Eve. Some of them are old friends from St. Louis, where I was the Nighthawk for many years on KTRS. Others are friends from *Coast,* who always like the Open Lines format. And tonight, as everyone listening gathers around the digital fireplace to share memories and stories of miracles and wonders, we talk about what people want to talk about in our radio community that stretches from the Pacific to the Atlantic and around the world. We talk about the supernatural and whether it's real or a figment of our collective imagination.

GEORGE'S EXPERIENCES WITH THE PARANORMAL

I practice what I preach in Worker in the Light. *In life, I rely heavily on intuition even to the extent that it overrides logic. For example, every night on the air, I can almost sense when there is a highly emotional caller in the bank of waiting calls. Of course my producer, Tom, is a call screener. Most talk radio shows have them. But sometimes*

I will sense something about a caller that isn't apparent at all. For example, I get a lot of calls about people who have been visited by departed loved ones. I mean a lot of calls. If you spend a night listening to Open Lines on Coast, you will hear some of the most poignant stories of callers who have lost a parent, a child, or a spouse who tell you that the loved one's voice will turn up on an answering machine from out of nowhere. How does my caller know it's his or her loved one? Sometimes the voice will say something that only the loved one will know. And, in just that one moment, the warmth of life will replace the chill of death. I know when this type of caller is on the line and I look forward to taking that call.

In the same way, I can feel the emotional stress from my own loved ones. I broadcast principally from Los Angeles, in our Sherman Oaks studio, two thousand miles or so away from my family. I have my parents in Detroit, my children, and grandchildren in St. Louis. I try to make it back to St. Louis during the year to be with them, but I have to be in L.A. So there are times when I get an overwhelming feeling of emotion or stress. It will come on me early in the morning in L.A., just as I'm trying to get to sleep. It will come on me on waking up in the bright sunshine or as I'm driving along one of the boulevards in the San Fernando Valley or in Beverly Hills. And when it comes on me, oftentimes I'll just pull the car over, throw a quarter in the meter, flip open my cell phone, and call the member of my family who, I believe, is transmitting a stressful message. Most often I'm right. I'll get a "Dad, I was just thinking about you." And I know that my intu-ition mechanism, the very mechanism I'm suggesting that you hone, is working.

So when I call my child or parent, I will be there to help even before they call me. All they have to do is think about it and I'm there, on the phone if not in person.

"Tell us the Ouija board story again," one caller says.

"Tell us about when you floated above your body," another wants to know.

"Is remote viewing really real?" yet another caller asks.

"Remote viewing. That's as good a place as any to start," I say to the caller. "Sit back. It's going to be a fun Christmas Eve."

"What do my experiences with the Ouija board, my out-of-body experience, and my experiment with the dark side have to do with remote viewing?" I say to the audience. "Essentially, two things."

Here is what they are. First, all three of these experiences showed me that there is an alternate reality, just as palpable as the three-dimensional reality within which we all navigate, but invisible to us unless we attune our senses to perceive it. Second, that there are gateways into this alternate reality, portals that allow anyone, whether psychic or not, to cross over into a reality where those who enter discover a part of themselves that allows them to wield untold powers over space and time. If you understand this and can use these gateways, you will become a more powerful, more understanding, and more loving creature. It will help you deal with other people in benevolent ways, and help you understand more about yourself and others than you can ever imagine. I sensed this very thing when my mind defied gravity and allowed me to leave my own body. And over the years it has given me the skill to work with different people in life and on the radio.

Part of me said that what I had experienced during my out-of-body event was a physical manifestation of something I didn't fully understand. I believed I knew what happened, but not why. I believed I had experienced something, but was it something that other people could experience? And if other people could experience it, was there a science behind it, a testable phenomenon that could be demonstrated to a skeptical public? Worse, if I could levitate myself, was I the kind of person who would have been persecuted during the time when witches were burned at the stake in Colonial New England?

This goal, the proof of an alternate reality, the discovery of a "science" underlying human spirituality, the development of evidence attesting to a fact that human beings are more than bones and flesh, became a quiet but persistent force in my life even as I completed college, served in the U.S. Navy, and launched into a career in broadcasting. What a happy surprise it was to me, therefore, that after I began my career as a talk show host and researched this alternate reality, I also found out that the United States military and intelligence services had not only discovered this reality over forty years ago, but it reverse- X engineered—that is to say, provided a hard-science basis for a psychic event—the process of entering an alternate reality so as to obtain funding from Congress and then trained officers to carry out spy missions in this invisible world. This military program, what the former members have called "psychic spying," was officially called "remote viewing." And it is there, with remote viewing, that most of the U.S. government–approved evidence for what I was attempting to discover on my own was already laid out.

There is some mystery surrounding the beginnings of the remote viewing program. Although U.S. Navy Commander L. R. Bremseth's 2001 "Asymmetric Warfare Implications of Remote Viewing," a report he compiled for the Marine Corps War College, talks about the beginnings of the program in the late 1960s, when U.S. intelligence services became aware of Soviet experiments with psychic spying, Lieutenant Colonel Philip J. Corso, in *The Day After Roswell*, intimates that our efforts at psychic warfare began even earlier. In describing a concern of his commanding officer, Lieutenant General Arthur Trudeau in 1961, Corso reveals that Trudeau said he had received intelligence that the Soviets were experimenting with psychokinesis to alter the trajectories of incoming Soviet ICBM warheads sitting within multiple reentry vehicles. Even a small alteration in the trajectory, Trudeau explained, would have catastrophic consequences for civil defense planners. Therefore, Trudeau asked Corso to write a report for him assessing the potential success of training psychics to counter the Soviet psychics by diverting incoming warheads from their targets to less populated areas or even out to sea. This might have been one of the early strategic planning sessions in the U.S.-Soviet Psy War.

According to another military officer, however, U.S. awareness of the power of what would become remote viewing began even earlier. Commander George Hoover, according to a naval response to an inquiry about what is referred to as the Philadelphia Experiment, was one of two officers who reviewed Morris K. Jessup's book, *The Case for the UFO*. In that book, Jessup writes about an incident that allegedly took place at the Philadelphia Navy Yard in October 1943, when the destroyer escort USS *Eldridge,* having been subjected to an intense electrical charge administered in an attempt to degauss her hull, vanished into a time portal. The Office of Naval Research, trying to respond to requests for information about this incident, as reported in the book, asked Commander George Hoover to research the event and provide comments to the Jessup narrative about the entire affair. The result was an annotated edition of the Jessup book, written by George Hoover. That book has all but disappeared, according to Navy records.

However, George Hoover himself became fascinated with the theories of time travel, out-of-body projection, and remote viewing and researched the field heavily, along with a goodly dose of UFO research. By the time he had retired from the Navy and had done consulting work for such companies as Walt Disney studios, George Hoover had become a bona fide expert on such things as UFOs, out-of-body experiences, and the possibilities of time travel. Commander Hoover said that within the inner circle of those members of the military who knew that we had been visited by extraterrestrials, the big secret wasn't the flying saucers themselves. By the time he had retired from the Navy, flying saucers were almost old hat to many people in the military intelligence services. The big secret, the one that really had to be covered up, he said, was the fact that not only extraterrestrials, but human beings, had the power of psychic projection, psychokinesis, and even time travel itself. It was an untapped power in our own brains, which we did not know how to utilize unless we were trained to perceive our own abilities. Intuitively, we could tap into it. But our need to navigate within a world of social hierarchies, order, and language obscured this power from us. Nevertheless, the power was there, and the military had begun a program to train officers in different forms of psychic projection as far back as the 1960s.

In the late 1960s, the United States became concerned about what they perceived as a "psy gap" between the United States and the Soviet Union. According to Ingo Swann, in an interview with Commander Bremseth, it became apparent to U.S. intelligence officials that the Soviets had, during the 1960s, at least, begun experimenting with various forms of psychic energy, forms of psychokinesis or mind control that could influence distant objects. Whether this remote influence was what Lieutenant General Arthur Trudeau was worried about when he asked Lieutenant Colonel Corso about the feasibility of using psychokinesis to alter our antimissile trajectories or not, by the end of the decade, Soviet experimentation was on the minds of the military intelligence community.

There was an additional concern, Commander Bremseth reported, involving the types of Soviet personnel who seemed to be behind the Soviet research, or at least were supporting it. Our intelligence services discovered that the KGB and GRU (Soviet military intelligence) were "controlling" the research, leading U.S. intelligence analysts to suspect that not only were the Soviets deadly serious about their commitment to parapsychological warfare, they expected real, tangible results. Whatever the game was, our side believed, it was a game we had to play. And if we didn't have the resources on the playing field at that moment, we had to get them there—and fast. Accordingly, what had once been relegated to New Age spiritualistic woo-woo became a crash program both for the military and the CIA. Civilian and military services found themselves in a game of third-quarter catch-up with scientists from the country that had been one of the founders of behavioral science.

But where to begin?

According to Paul H. Smith's history of the Army's remote viewing program in *Reading the Enemy's Mind* (Tor/Forge, 2005) as well Commander Bremseth's interview with Stanford Research Institute's Hal Puthoff, which he refers to in his report, Puthoff, a former Naval Intelligence offer, had been working with artist Ingo Swann, observing his extraordinary psychic abilities. Puthoff was hardly New Age. He was a physicist who had experimented with lasers. He had been a part of the hunt for the elusive zero-point energy, seeking to identify, isolate, and harvest a form of energy lurking amid the dark matter of space that most people thought was only a theory and a tenuous one at that. But Puthoff had become impressed with Swann's abilities and had written a report about his observations to the CIA.

Coming at a time when our intelligence services couldn't afford to take a possible Soviet threat lightly, the Agency was so intrigued by what Puthoff had written, that they shared their concerns with him. They had been tracking the Soviet experiments since 1962, the same time period during which Trudeau and Corso were still at Army research and development. But the question that had to be answered was whether Ingo Swann's skills could be utilized for military intelligence purposes. And if they could be, could whatever skills Swann possessed be nurtured in others.

Bremseth writes that "Puthoff invited Swann to visit SRI . . . to investigate the boundary between the animate and inanimate." In other words, would Swann be able to exercise his psychic powers in such a way that he could affect changes in physical objects—psychokinesis? To test out this possibility, Puthoff set up a blind test in which he encouraged Swann, while they were touring SRI's laboratories, to demonstrate his psychic powers by viewing the facility's heavily shielded magnetometer. The device had to be heavily shielded because it was used to measure the incidence of quarks. Not only was Swann able to view the device, he was able to draw an internal diagram of it. At the same time that Swann was viewing it, however, the device itself began measuring a magnetic field that had suddenly been switched on out of nowhere. That magnetic field, it turned out, was the physical manifestation of Swann's viewing the very sensitive device from outside the device's shielding. What this event seemed to indicate was that the act of remote viewing had a very real presence of physical energy, a type of signal that could be picked up and measured, a type of signal that was clearly generated, directed, and received. For skeptics who dismiss psychic events as pure fantasy, this one instance, as described by Puthoff and Swann, and reported by Bremseth, is enough to show that there is a reality to it perhaps unseen by most people but nevertheless scientifically measurable and verifiable.

Swann's performance was so persuasive, especially when he repeated the test, that the CIA began funding a research project to ascertain the feasibility of remote viewing and also see whether people could be trained to remote view. In these tests, as Russell Targ has written (Stanford: Society for Scientific Exploration, Journal of Scientific Exploration, Vol. 10, no. 1, as cited by Bremseth), and as described by both Ingo Swann and Hal Puthoff, an individual would travel to a location selected at random outside the laboratory and a remote viewer would be tasked to describe where the person was. When the session was completed, the viewer and other experimenters would go to the location to see whether the viewer's verbal and written impressions were accurate. Puthoff said that in order to safeguard the scientific accuracy of the testing procedures themselves, the CIA had monitors inside the program making sure that nobody was faking the results.

Paul H. Smith, who was one of Ingo Swann's original trainees in coordinate remote viewing (CRV), recalls in his book, *Reading the Enemy's Mind,* that after the initial experiments, the program planners expanded the program to scanning by geographical coordinates. At first, the coordinates were the coordinates given to the remote viewers by their monitors. However, the program managers realized that the viewers could gauge where they were supposed to go simply by figuring out what the latitude and longitude coordinates referred to. So to avoid any outside influences and interferences, and to validate the entire testing and training mechanism, the monitors were provided with random numbers to give to the remote viewers. Thus, at one point in the training, not even the monitors knew where the locations were because the numbers they had were random.

If all this sounds like mumbo jumbo to you, think about how it sounded to the bureaucrats in the intelligence command and those in the legislative loop who were being asked to cough up funding for the program. How do you explain to a legislator on the House Intelligence Subcommittee, for example, a legislator from a very conservative district, that you want that person to vote funds for a program that purports to send psychics to project their vision into the ether where they will be able to pass through walls and probe into locked file cabinets to rifle through enemy secrets? If this seems like an impossible hurdle, think of what it might have seemed like thirty years ago, before the collapse of the Soviet Union. Consequently, the remote-viewing program managers, and Ingo Swann and Hal Puthoff in particular, Paul Smith told us in an interview, had to figure out a way to make this projection of vision into hard science. As we wrote in our *UFO Magazine* interview with Smith in 2004, Puthoff and Swann had to find a way to "reverse engineer" remote viewing to make it into a science that any House or Senate budget committee overseer would love.

On first look, that seemed to be a significant challenge. Although Ingo Swann could make the dial on a magnetometer flip around and Uri Geller, another well-known psychic, could use the power of his mind to bend metal, what other proof was there? Using what amounted to party tricks to prove the viability of a potential military weapon, especially in Cold War America, wasn't nearly enough to show that remote viewing was based on a hard science and not just the special sixth-sense talents of a few individuals. Therefore, as Paul Smith told us, the onus fell on Puthoff and Swann to make a case for hard science.

First was the issue of the trainability of this skill. Did a remote viewer have to be truly gifted, in the small percentile of human beings who could harness a perception beyond the five senses? If so, then look for kinds of psychics floating in the pool in *Minority Report*, the Cassandras of ancient mythology, the Oracle at Delphi who foretold the future. Or, as Paul Smith suggested to us, was this a skill that can be taught to anyone, just like playing the piano? You didn't have to be a Van Cliburn to plunk out a simple melody that anyone could sing to at a party. You simply had to know what keys to play when. It would have to be just such a skill in order for it to pass the trainability test. Sure, some individuals would score higher on the tests than others and some would exercise greater skill and perception. But, if this were to become a form of spying, it had to be teachable.

Second was the issue of hard science. Ingo Swann himself has said that the proof of remote viewing is simply that it works. It is its own proof of its existence. But, twenty-five years ago things weren't so simple. What is the hard science that can explain something so evanescent as mentally projecting one's perception to a distant place in order to see things in a detail that will allow an intelligence operation to be conducted there? This was a question that not only required an answer, it required a scientific theory to explain it. And Paul Smith described to us how Ingo Swann helped developed a theory that would turn paranormal into simply normal and ultimately allow for the funding of what otherwise would have been just another form of New Age channeling.

First there was no shortage of theories to explain what remote viewing did. It could be a type of perception only, the training of someone to perceive things that were physically there but not apparent to the untrained eye. But this explanation fell far short of the all-encompassing theory sought. Alternatively, if one looked at it simply as an act of information retrieval from a vast database of all human existence, theories to explain it went as far back as ancient mythology, shamans, and the Bible. Most recently, the nineteenth-century Theosophists and Madame Blavatsky were proponents of a universal storehouse of all knowledge from which visitors could partake. But such theories also implied a judgmental aspect to the process, and Ingo Swann was looking for a nonjudgmental component. Remote viewers shouldn't have to assess what they were seeing because that leads to misperceptions, to logical interference with raw data, to an analysis that may misinterpret what's being viewed. Thus, judgment had to be eliminated from the initial stages of the process.

What kind of theory, therefore, could Ingo Swann have developed to explain his technique of training viewers to eliminate an analytical overlay of the perception? Could there be a model for the reality of remote viewing that would satisfy scientists, yet operate within the realm of political acceptability as well, if it had to, because it was grounded securely in physics? Ultimately, the answer was yes. As Paul Smith reveals, Swann and Puthoff turned to something very old and then to something very new.

In order for remote viewing to satisfy the budget folks who make the funding decisions, the process had to be grounded in a material science. That is, it had to be as physical as a jet engine. It had to be tangible reality, not alternate reality. But how do you describe something as intangible as the projection of one's senses to distant places while the body remains in one place? You can't unless you ascribe to the events that remote viewers perceive a material substance that anyone can perceive. In order to do this, Paul Smith told us, the early formulations of a theory had to with the ancient Platonic notion of a universe of forms that imparted a corresponding tangibleness to the things we see in our everyday world. So for a table, there was the form of a table that existed somewhere in the universe and from which ideal form every table that ever existed took essence. Everybody who ever took Philosophy 101 read Plato, so that was a pretty good start.

But it also left much to be desired as a theory because we

weren't just describing tables and chairs, viewers were traveling to remote places, hearing sounds, smelling smells. There had to be something more encompassing as a theory, something that operated more in the realm of physical reality. What Hal Puthoff and Ingo Swann developed next were ideas from physicist David Bohm's *Wholeness and the Implicate Order,* in which Bohm suggests, according to Smith, that the implicate order is "a strange domain involving atomic and subatomic particles and their often bizarre interactions." In these reactions, not only can particles become waves as a result of the simple act of external observation, but they have a "virtual existence," where particles can wink in and out of existence without violating the laws of physics. And even more critical for the remote-viewing theorists was the principle of nonlocality, "the principle whereby influence can be exerted between particles across time and space instantaneously and without any intervening forces." Smith describes this theory, an essential component of applied quantum physics, in *Reading the Enemy's Mind.*

Imagine a force, say the power of thought, for example, that can flip one particle and a corresponding particle flips elsewhere in the universe. Here, the instantaneous nature of this influence even exceeds the speed of light and defies what most people might call causality. Thus, it's not as though particle A causes the the instant alteration of particle B; they simply happen at the same time. Imagine that two particles, perhaps separated by millions of miles in space and millions of years along our time continuum, simply flip at the same instant as if one particle were influencing another. But it's the speed of transmission that is an essential element of this process as well. As

Philip J. Corso once said, the thing that always impressed him about the possibilities of remote viewing was that the speed of thought was instantaneous—well beyond the speed of light.

What did all this have to do with remote viewing? Ingo Swann said that "The explicate [order of real objects and things] and the implicate order are available to human consciousness at all times. People focus on the explicate order [the things we see in our everyday existence] but never focus on the implicate order." It was part of the underlying theory of remote viewing that the implicate order, as an aggregate of a particle collective, operated as the basis of an existence of a database of all things living and nonliving, a database where everything resides and inside which nothing is destroyed. It is this database, the matrix, from which remote viewers can retrieve the information about their targets. The locations of the targets are either in the minds of the monitors managing the remote viewing session, or in the minds of the managers who give the randomly selected coordinates to the monitors. Either way, the viewers are supposedly blind to the actual locations and only use the random number coordinates as a springboard to find the carrier signal and journey into the matrix.

This version of a matrix of all things in the universe was, Paul Smith said, conceived by Ingo Swann, whose original hypothesis described it as an "infinity of information points." Each point was roughly equivalent to a specific coordinate on a cosmic hard drive containing the stored sum of information from all things that ever existed, continue to exist, and will exist. The same database houses all things, past, present, and possible future. In this realm, all potential futures exist simultaneously along with the paths that lead to them. Paul Smith told us that part of the training process was teaching someone how to perceive without interference from that person's analytical side of the brain so as to note all of the impressions in a nonjudgmental way. All people, to a greater or lesser extent, had the ability to be trained. And the training was in the methodology of letting impressions get through without the static of everyday existence. Thus trained, anyone could be a remote viewer.

Swann's and Puthoff's scientific model worked even at these early stages, and allowed practitioners to conceive of remote viewing not as a trip to a specific target but as a retrieval of information from the matrix where all information about the target was stored. It was simply a process of accessing the cosmic hard drive by means of acquiring a mental signal line, a kind of carrier wave on which resided the bits of data that made their way into the minds of remote viewers.

For those trained in remote viewing, the actual perception or decoding of the psychic data takes place within the subconscious mind, below the threshold of consciousness. The signal is picked up right away, but the process of homing in on the details of the object, filtering out the everyday reality chatter so as to let the perceptions of the target resolve themselves, is gradual, even though the signal connection is almost instantaneous. The staging process is important because the danger even for experienced remote viewers is to let the judgment facilities resident in the left hemisphere of the brain jump on the perceptions that are forming and come to conclusions. These conclusions, called analytical overlays by Ingo Swann and company, distort what the remote viewer sees and replace it with conclusory statements that can be very misleading.

The overwhelming majority of people, the theory of remote viewing posits, live their lives completely in the conscious mind, decoding signals from the everyday world so as to navigate their separate ways through life. We all stop at red lights, pick up a ringing telephone, pull our fingers back from sharp objects, prop our feet up on a cushion or ottoman, and savor a hot cup of coffee in the morning. We plop ourselves into a chair and expect not to fall down. We put a car into drive and feel the transmission engage. We expect to go forward, not back up. In short, we live in a world of sensations and physical impressions that conform to our expectations of what will happen. We preset conditions for what and how our actions will result and are often stunned when the most mundane of expectations don't turn out the way they're supposed to. For most of us, if the world of the subconscious intrudes, it is a very psychologically uncomfortable feeling because we've shoved stuff into our subconscious that we'd rather not deal with on the everyday level. But what about those people who know how to live in the subconscious or who have been trained to respond to subconscious signals in addition to conscious ones? What about people who are like the psychics in *Minority Report,* shielded from everyday sensations that disturb the delicate reception of images in their subconscious minds?

For people self-trained in the practice of remote viewing, and for people who know how to tune into their subconscious minds, the carrier signal to the matrix of all things living and nonliving is much stronger and can be acquired more quickly. These people may be more sensitive to potential futures, more driven by what they call "instinct" than real-world logic, and may even talk about having ESP. Maybe these people are already in communication with the matrix, picking up a signal with data of a very different kind than people who shut out their subconscious minds.

The formal training process in controlled or coordinate re-mote viewing (CRV), Paul Smith explained to us, teaches the practice of keying off the coordinates, listening to the messages forming in the subconscious, allowing them to be observed without analytical intervention so as to withhold levying a judgment on them, and deliberately keeping these impressions out of a conscious structure. In other words, this is a psychic voyage into the matrix to view the assemblage of a particular constellation of particles. This was the kind of training candidates for the Defense Intelligence Agency remote-viewing program went through when Paul Smith was invited to join.

In the coordinate remote viewing manual Paul Smith wrote for the military, he describes the matrix and the process of reaching it this way:

> The Matrix has been described as a huge, non-material, highly structured, mentally accessible "framework" of information containing all data pertaining to everything in both the physical and non-physical universe. In the same vein as Jung's Cosmic Unconsciousness, the Matrix is open to and comprises all conscious entities as well as information relating to everything else living or nonliving by accepted human definition. It is this informational framework from which the data encoded on the signal line originates. This Matrix can be envisioned as a vast, three dimensional geometric arrangement of dots, each dot representing a discrete information bit. Each geographic location on the earth has a corresponding segment of the Matrix corresponding exactly to the nature of the physical location. When the viewer is prompted by the coordinate or other targeting methodol-

ogy, he accesses the signal line for data derived from the Matrix. By successfully acquiring (detecting) this information from the signal line, then coherently decoding it through his conscious awareness and faculties, he makes it available for analysis and further exploitation by himself or others.

Remote viewing is made possible through the agency of a hypothetical "signal line." In a manner roughly analogous to standard radio propagation theory, this signal line is a carrier wave which is inductively modulated by its intercourse with information and may be detected and decoded by a remote viewer. This signal line radiates in many different frequencies, and its impact on the viewer's perceptive faculties is controlled through a phenomenon known as "aperture." Essentially, when the remote viewer first detects the signal line in Stage I it manifests itself as a sharp, rapid influx of signal energy—representing large gestalts of information. In this situation, we therefore speak of a "narrow" aperture, since only a very narrow portion of the signal line is allowed to access the consciousness. In later stages involving longer, slower, more enduring waves, the aperture is spoken of as being "wider."

If the matrix model works and if particles separated from each other can influence their respective states, is there a theory that might explain how all of this happened, how past, present, and all potential futures can coexist, and how it could have been presented scientifically in such a way that a legislator's chief of staff or a member of the Senate Armed Services Committee might feel comfortable in making a budget recommendation for funding? In Paul Smith's theory, just such a scientific model exists to explain how the matrix might have been created and even why there might be relationships between particles in the cosmos such that one particle's activity might influence its corresponding particle.

Assume for the sake of argument that the big-bang theorists are correct and that there was a moment, or an eternity, before time itself began to tick away when all matter in the universe—even its form as energy—was compressed into a point so small it might not have been perceivable even had someone been around to see it. The point was so small it was actually dimensionless. Everything that today comprises the entire universe was compressed into that point, forming a great, uncomfortably claustrophobic, link of all existence. This was the matrix at a state before time, a state before matter itself began to decay, a state before entropy entered the vocabulary of the universe. In that state, there was complete locality, a micromatrix with all existence compressed into a single dot— amid what? Emptiness? And then, for whatever reason—a repellant magnetic force? internal pressure from the concentration of all this matter? maybe even centrifugal force from the tight spin of the singularity?—there was an explosion of all this compressed energy/matter. It was then that the bits and pieces of what was to become the universe flew apart from one another, just as they are flying apart from one another to this very day.

However, who is to say the link that once existed among every bit of matter no longer exists? What if the energy that bound all that matter together before the beginning of time still binds all that matter together, only it is stretched across what looks like, but probably is not, an emptiness of space? The relationships among all aspects of existence and the fabric of time itself could simply be this microdot of the universe made huge over the course of billions of years. Might this, then, be the very foundation of the matrix Ingo Swann described when he and Hal Puthoff formulated their scientific theories to explain how and why remote viewing works? It's a tantalizing possibility and was apparently good enough science to have kept the conveyor belt of government funding coming in until corporate America caught on and figured the best way for Macy's to find out what Gimbels was up to was by remote viewing what was going into the window displays for Christmas.

The additional big secret was that remote viewing was eminently trainable. Almost anyone could be taught to do it—you, your friends, your children, and even, as Ingo Swann found out, those who were or could turn out to be your enemies. As Ingo Swann described it in his book, *Penetration,* he might have thought he was remote-viewing structures in outer space, but he almost freaked out when he discovered that the aliens he had spotted were already remote viewing him. Like Frodo's ring in Tolkien's Lord of the Ring trilogy that made Frodo visible to Sauron even though he was invisible to everyone else, once a remote viewer followed the carrier signal to the matrix and thence to the target, the viewer himself became visible to other entities who could track him.

So, if you take the trouble to train yourself in remote viewing, tell yourself to imagine you are bathed in a white light wherever you go. The light will protect you from those who will see you in another dimension, which is what Ingo Swann says happened to him. Follow the advice of those who've been there before and make sure you're not being followed across another dimension.

Process and
Time Travel

I f you ever have the opportunity to observe a remote viewing session, such as those in the Jim Marrs's video, *The Secrets of Redgate,* you will notice that the viewers seem to be reporting impressions, visual as well as auditory, and that they don't seem to come to any conclusions or judgments. To the uninitiated watching these session or reading these reports, it can seem frustrating. They might question, "Don't these people know what they're seeing? It's a [fill in the blank]." But being purely observant and nonjudgmental is exactly what remote viewers are taught to do. Coming to premature conclusions is a no-no because once you apply analysis to a perception, you can be tricked into going down the wrong path and reporting the wrong thing. Spies, for example, and reporters, are told not to apply judgments to what they see. They are told to report only what they see and let the judgments come later.

In their training, remote viewers are taught that impressions will not come into their minds full-blown. Rather, they practice focusing or tuning in on the signal line—the mentalistic carrier signal that runs from the mind of the person who selected the target to the matrix of all existence. This should be a particularly rich signal, so viewers early in their training have to imbue themselves with it gradually. They accomplish this by scalloping into the signal by stages. Level by level, they allow themselves to perceive more, focus on what they have perceived, and allow themselves to pick up more impressions. The methodology, remote viewers have said, is to train the viewer not to allow him or herself to become overwhelmed. The impressions can be so vivid that the brain's recticular window, the window of sensory perception, can become flooded with images that crash in on each other and disable the viewer's ability to describe them. Rather, the viewer is taught to report on the broad outlines of a scene, discrete shapes and colors, jotting down impressions on a piece of paper as they come in. Then the viewer reports on more refined images, including sounds, until a picture emerges.

Were you to look at a viewer's notes of a session, you would see series of recorded impressions that become more and more specific, stage by stage, until the final stage when the viewer allows himself to comment on where he has been and what he's seen. Maybe the viewer's conclusions will be incorrect, as were Paul Smith's when he was given the coordinates for Hiroshima moments after the nuclear detonation but believed that he might have been at the site of a volcanic eruption, but the impressions themselves still remain. And because the viewer's target is not a mystery to the handler or the person who chose the target in the first place, it's the impressions that matter more to the viewer than where the viewer believed he has been, because only the handler or targeter knows the actual destination.

Because the viewer is directed not to jump to conclusions about what he or she is perceiving, leaving any judgments to the very end, if necessary, viewers sometimes actually don't know where they've been until the session is over, or know actually what they've seen. Thus, when a remote viewer actually travels in time as well as space, when he perceives a target, it is often as much of a mystery at first as what the actual target is.

On its face, the mere concept of remote perception time

travel must have been stunning to the managers of the remote viewing program. Granted, for psychics and individuals who possess the gift of foresight, the implications of viewing the future might not have been particularly overwhelming. In fact, I imagine they might have been more burdensome than anything else. Consider Cassandra, for example. Here she was, at the outset of the Trojan War while preparations were being made for the heroic defense of a magnificent city, predicting the ultimate downfall of the kingdom and the defeat of her people. As the story goes, it did not make her the most popular person in Troy. Can the same be said for others whose gift of prescience has made for unfortunate predictions?

But individuals who are gifted with second sight or the ability of prognostication, and have accepted their abilities, often tend to immunize themselves against the stigma that historically goes along with this by simply keeping what they see to themselves. Or they go the other route and commercialize it in such a way that even dire predictions don't get them into trouble. As author Joel Martin has written, some professional seers, when confronting a particularly horrendous event in the future, such as the assassination of John F. Kennedy, have kept their thoughts to themselves. An exception was Jean Dixon who had said that she repeatedly tried to get a message to President Kennedy not to go to Dallas, but that her attempts were unsuccessful.

Jean Dixon was one of the more respected professional prognosticators. Others, depending on from whence they claim their gift of foresight, may meet with various degrees of disdain and thus their dire predictions are taken less than seriously except by those who are true believers in the seers themselves. Such has been the case with some UFO contactees who report that their interactions with extraterrestrials have provided them with information about the future by the time-traveling or extradimensional ETs, that they, the contactees, have been allowed to bring back to human beings. These cases, and the cases of the prophets who report to the tabloid newspapers, are instances of "commercial" time travel.

The idea of time travel, while theoretically included in the premise of a matrix of all things living and nonliving, was still significant enough to have made an impression on the remote viewers when its practical nature was revealed to them. As Paul Smith told us in our interview, he discovered the practical applications of time travel when, about twenty years ago, he remote-viewed an event in the Persian Gulf during the Iran-Iraq War when the U.S. Navy was protecting all American-flagged tankers. Major Smith received the impressions of a metallic vessel on water, a craft of some sort moving through the air, and a place inland where men in uniform were controlling some sort of event. He also perceived another craft in the air, watching the entire event unfold. The craft controlled by the men inland, men wearing brown uniforms, launched a cylindrical object. It was moving rapidly toward the vessel on the water. Men in the vessel were aware of the object moving toward them. They could do nothing about it. There was a sense of unreality, then of panic. Then the cylindrical object struck. There was the screeching sound of metal, then fire, then the acrid wretchedness of burning flesh.

The men inland at first were overjoyed at something, then they, too, experienced panic. Something had gone horribly wrong with what they were planning. Some of the sailors in the vessel, now barely afloat and beginning to sink, were hurt.

There was pandemonium as crews went to extinguish the fires. Meanwhile, personnel in the larger craft overhead—it turned out to be a Saudi AWACS plane—tried to dispatch interceptors to bring down the attacking plane, but were too late. On the vessel, the explosion had blown a hole in the hull and had mangled and melted part of the superstructure. But the vessel, now listing to port, was able to stay afloat. The remote viewing session ended. It was a Friday afternoon.

Paul Smith wrote up his notes for the session and went home for the weekend, not really knowing what event he had specifically perceived. It was obviously an attack on a Navy ship by a plane that had fired a missile at it, but that was all that could be determined. Very early on Monday morning, Major Smith received a call to get to his supervisor's office as quickly as he could. Once there, he watched as his supervisor picked up his report, held it out, and asked whether this report was as accurate as it could be. Smith said yes. Then his supervisor turned over a copy of Monday morning's *Washington Post*. On it was the banner headline, "Iraqi Warplane Attacks USS *Stark*." The lead story described how an Iraqi fighter launched two Exocet missiles at the Navy destroyer USS *Stark*, one of which detonated and caused a fire amidships that almost sank the vessel. It was the exact event that Major Smith had remote-viewed. Only there was one problem. Paul Smith had remote-viewed the event forty-eight hours before it took place.

There were other instances, Major Smith told us, that he realizes today might have been instances of remote viewing into the future. But the attack on USS *Stark* that was very telling because, if you put yourself in the remote viewer's position, you should be asking what exactly you had seen. Was it an event that was destined to happen, locked into the future? Was it an event that was going to happen absent any intervention on your or anyone's part? Were you, by remote viewing it, now a part of the history of the future? Had Paul Smith known exactly what he was remote viewing and that it was an attack that had not taken place, what should have been his responsibility? Should he have done his best to get a warning to the USS *Stark* that they would be attacked in the Gulf? Would the Stark have activated its Phalanx antimissile shield so as to shoot down the incoming Exocet once it was acquired on radar? Should the United States have gotten the Saudis involved so that once their AWACS radar plane spotted the warplanes, allied fighters could have intercepted them?

These are all classic questions anyone would encounter if presented with the opportunity to travel, albeit psychically, into the future. Yet, this is not theory. The astounding fact is that the United States Army, over twenty years ago, discovered that within one of its own intelligence programs, personnel had stumbled onto a kind of time machine. They had discovered real time travel into the future via remote viewing. This was no joke, no New Age mystery tour, no unsubstantiated claim. And even if only one officer had accomplished this task, it meant that it was a task that was accomplishable. This was real, official, time travel into the future. The event perceived was not only palpable but logically foreseeable and eminently preventable. The lingering question was, what did it mean?

I can't stress enough how important Paul Smith's remote viewing session was because it is decidedly not a fluke and shows, definitively, that a future event can be perceived. This incident, and I don't know if anyone can say for sure how many times and in how many different contexts it was repeated, goes to the very heart of the theory of remote viewing. It presupposes that what Ingo Swann theorized about a matrix of all things living and nonliving certainly exists in some way, shape, or form. Also, until Steven Hawking reversed a major component of his own theory of black holes, it was a clear indication that Hawking was wrong. Hawking had said that when matter, whether in the form of energy or mass, slips into a black hole, it doesn't reemerge but disappears forever. At a conference earlier in 2004, however, Professor Hawking reversed himself and said that he had reformulated his theory of black holes and come to the conclusion that matter does not disappear. All information in the universe remains in the universe and is not swallowed up by black holes. In fact, he said that even if information reemerges on the other side of the black hole, it remains intact. All information remains forever. In one swoop, the Hawking theory of black holes and perpetual existence of information, the Ingo Swann theory of the matrix of all things living and nonliving, and even the Platonic theory of a world of forms imparting meaning and shape to a world of reflections on the walls of the cave of life all unify.

Therefore, what this means is not only that remote viewing and time travel are real phenomena, which is a stunning thought in and of itself, but that there is a real universe out there, an "uber universe" in which all things that were, are, or can be actually exist and can be visited by anyone with the proper training.

The moral implications of this phenomena are enormous. Just think of the burden borne by those who can navigate in this universe. If you were Major Paul Smith, for example, and realized what was happening and had been able to identify the vessel and its location, would you have moved heaven and earth to warn the captain and its crew? What do you think would happen as you tried to explain to your superiors in the Pentagon that you had just traveled in time—a secret weapon whose existence you've just revealed—where you saw an attack on a U.S. Navy warship in the Persian Gulf by a supposed ally while another supposed ally using your own AWACS plane cruised overhead and sat on its backside until it was too late to shoot down the attacking plane? Imagine the collective expression of derision by people in the upper echelons of the Pentagon as you tried to explain what was about to take place and how you knew about it as the hours ticked away. Would you get increasingly frustrated as your warnings, like those of a Cassandra, fell on deaf ears? Would you buck the chain of command and take matters into your own hands? Sounds like the plot of a great motion picture, doesn't it, Tom Cruise or John Travolta seething with fury as the Iraqis calmly fueled up their jets on Monday morning, Gulf time, as they prepared for their practice run at the American warship?

Maybe you would be successful, get the warning through so that the warship changed direction. Maybe your warning would have been the trigger for the confusion that resulted in the ship's antimissile defenses not being activated. You, then, would be the direct and proximate cause of the injuries on the defenseless ship. How can you extrapolate the results of your actions when you can time travel into the future? Do you ask yourself, as Ebenezer Scrooge asked the Ghost of Christmas Future, whether these are only the shadows of things to come that can be changed by our actions in the present or are these things unalterable, destined to be? Or do you take the approach of the Federation of Planets from *Star Trek* and impose a prime directive on all time travelers: "Do not interfere with the future or with the past under any circumstances." These are problems complicated enough to make an ethicist cross-eyed.

It's intriguing to think that this problem has already been encountered. The Army, although it never announced it in a headline the way it announced the retrieval of a crashed flying saucer in 1947 from outside of Roswell, has indeed had to wrestle with this or deny its existence. Maybe it made believe it was just some sort of an anomaly and didn't want to offend the conservative-thinking members of the congressional budgetary committees who'd be reluctant to put taxpayer's money into some sort of time machine. Maybe the whole time travel file, and we know there is at least one report in it, went black. We know that the Stargate remote-viewing files were ultimately released to the public in 1995, when the remote-viewing project was ostensibly shut down. Where it went after that, I cannot say. However, what is intriguing is the trail of breadcrumbs left by Ingo Swann in his books about the remote-viewing project and the exciting things he had to say about what he discovered.

In an eerie reminder of the Carlos Castaneda stories of Yaqui shaman Don Juan and the alternate realities of the Yaqui tribe Don Juan described, Swann revealed from his experience that while a remote viewer might be traveling to a distant place to perceive a target, maybe the viewer himself was the target of a strange being perceiving him. Is there a psychic superhighway across which human beings can project themselves, the express or passing lanes of which are also traveled by entities from other planets, realities, dimensions, or even universes?

And if so, are there physical off-ramps into our realities, exits into history or into a future that is a history for someone else? Ingo Swann explored these, he has said, on his travels to places where if there were extraterrestrial aliens they would most likely be.

CHAPTER

4

THE HUMANOIDS

How did it all start, George?" A caller on the Wild Card Line asks.

People are settling in for the long Christmas Eve now here in Los Angeles. But across the country, trees have been decorated, the kids are in bed, families are enjoying the final eggnog, coffee, or hot milk, and waiting for the sound of stirring early in the morning. But there are those who are alone who just want to talk. Especially for them my lines are open.

My caller takes my mind back to a different place and time. If you'd asked me what I wanted to be, way back almost forty years ago when I was a freshman at the University of Detroit, at a time when the Midwest was just waking up to the words of Dr. Timothy Leary and the lyrics of Jefferson Airplane, and when the rumblings of change and protest were rolling out of Berkeley, California, to listening posts in the heartland of America, I would have told you in one word: Dentist! Dentistry, the profession, ran in my family like a tradition and all of my relatives were dentists. My father was only too happy to see me join the profession. He had agreed to pay all the education bills. It would have been a great deal. There was only one problem. I wanted to be an actor even more.

My artistic proclivities notwithstanding, like a good soldier on a march I followed my relatives to the University of Detroit, where, for the first one and half years, I dutifully studied chemistry, organic chemistry, algebra, physics, and all the other requirements that any premed or predent freshman has to shoulder. But the dream of being an actor flickered inside me like a candle in the darkness. The thought of being involved in broadcasting in some way kept popping up over and over again, often right in the middle of solving an organic chemistry problem in lab while my lab partners glared at me as my pencil hung there, poised over the scratch paper.

Like the collective opprobrium of a Greek chorus, everyone told me I was supposed to be a dentist. But there was another part of me that wanted to work in entertainment or broadcasting. Plopping drops of orange or blue syrupy stuff through an eyedropper into a test tube just didn't turn me on. Also, I simply didn't want to follow the rest of the family into a profession that, while honorable, really held no passion for me. I wanted to be in broadcasting, preferably in front of the camera or microphone. My mind had been fixated on broadcasting ever since I was a kid.

What had captured my imagination about being on camera was a strange television character who ruled Detroit in the 1960s called "Dr. Morgus." His real name was Sid Noel, a writer with a predilection for science and scientific experimentation, who began his television career in New Orleans and bounced around different television stations. He was the host of a horror movie show on Detroit television and even starred in his own feature film, *The Wacky World of Dr. Morgus*. It was Morgus who got me interested in broadcasting. I would run home from school every day, not bothering to hang around with friends, because I wanted to get in front of the television in time to see Dr. Morgus on Channel 2. He would do the weather and do scientific experiments. I was already interested in the paranormal after my out-of-body experience when I was eleven or twelve. And here was a scientist on television playing the role of a ghoul host for some of those great 1930s to 1950s horror movies, combining his love of science with a passion for entertaining. He was my inspiration to seek a career in broadcasting. It got my juices going. I mentioned Sid on the air one night, saying that I had no idea where he was or what he was doing. A caller said that Sid was doing the same kind of show on Cox Cable in New Orleans. My producers contacted him and got him on my show. That was my first direct contact with him. After Hurricane Katrina, my producers flew him to L.A. to surprise me with his in-studio appearance on the show. It was the first time we met. Sid and I are friends to this day, and I continue to be amazed at the wealth of talent he has, not only as a television personality, but as a writer and scholar of the industry.

Influenced as I was by Dr. Morgus and by the lure of the microphone, in the middle of my sophomore year I came to a momentous decision that resulted in my father's not speaking to me for months. I decided to buck family tradition, give up the drill, the speculum, and the long sharp-tipped dental pick, and change my major to communications with a specialty in broadcasting. I was going to follow my dream, let my instincts lead me to the right path. I realized that if I just walked along a path well trodden by those who expected me to follow it, regardless of the financial success and security I might have had, I would have been desperate to explore other things. That desperation could have been ultimately destructive. And it's advice I often give: if your instinct is leading you along a certain path, you do no harm by exploring it even if you don't ultimately commit to it.

Dr. Shafica Karagulla

When I was growing up, my future was laid out for me. I would be a dentist, a health care professional. Thoughts of broadcasting on paranormal subjects, hosting an open mike talk show into the wee hours of the morning, was a far cry from what my parents wanted me to do. But even back then, my aunt, Dr. Shafica Karagulla was an important signpost for me. My aunt—I call her my aunt even though she was my father's distant cousin—and I shared the same fascination with the paranormal. She was of Middle Eastern Origin, a dark-haired woman with a very kindly face. She was a scientist and very thorough about her work. But mostly, she had a burning curiosity that drove her into places most medical doctors wouldn't dare explore. Imagine a female doctor in the 1950s, at a time when medicine was still male-dominated and very frightened about the unknown, especially the paranormal, who openly espoused views about a sensory perception that her colleagues couldn't see, hear, touch, or even measure. Aunt Shafica took a measuring stick to that form of sensory perception and demonstrated it.

She was a legend in our family and I wanted her to be proud of me even though I had met her only a few times, since she lived in Los Angeles, far away from us in Detroit, and her career and research kept her traveling and busy. I was a kid with dreams of broadcasting, even though my father wanted me to go to dental school. Yet, Shafica and I did talk, especially after I decided not to complete dental school and went into broadcasting instead. As I worked my way up the professional broadcasting ladder, from television news production into on-air radio talent, Shafica revealed a fascination with what I was doing. I always felt that she wanted me to cross my field in broadcasting with hers in the paranormal. I hope she would be proud of me now . . . because that's exactly what I did.

Instinct is often a good guide, even when logic tells you just the opposite. Sometimes you have to force logic to agree with your instinct to prove to others that you have chosen the right path. If logic overrides your honest instinct about something, maybe you're listening to the wrong message. Maybe, as Ingo Swann taught his remote-viewing students, the analytical overlay from one part of your brain is overriding a real truth that you are psychically following.

This was an important concept that was heavily stressed in the remote-viewing training. I draw the analogy between my own experience and the remote-viewing process just to show that if you have an instinctive sense about something and follow it, you reach a goal that may be more in keeping with what you really want than the goal you're told you want.

This was, in part, Ingo Swann's advice in his book, *Penetration,* where he explains his remote-viewing experiences in the context of his own theory that the logical everyday mind acts as an interference to what human beings are capable of really knowing. Swann taught his remote-viewing candidates, as Paul Smith describes in *Reading the Enemy's Mind,* that the enemy of intuitiveness was often the logical overlay that we put on everything we see and hear. By forcing our experiences to fit into boxes created by that logic or, worse, discounting anything that challenges that logic, we effectively cut ourselves off from an entire experiential universe because we have no way to categorize it. This categorization, branding, labeling, and shoehorning experiences and perceptions into logical pigeonholes was what Ingo Swann called the "analytical overlay" that was the death of the instant impressions viewers received from their psychic travels to the Jungian universe of all things living and nonliving, past, present, and future.

The possibility of analytical overlay became a central issue, challenging Ingo Swann's instinct about what he had perceived, during what became a frightening psychic trip to the lunar surface and an encounter with humanoid entities. Ingo's experiences and his trip to the moon all came about, he writes in *Penetration,* after a mysterious encounter with an individual who called himself "Axelrod," not his real name, of course. Axelrod contacted Ingo Swann, who was working with Harold Puthoff at the Stanford Research Institute, and thus began a "Spy vs. Spy" episode in which Ingo was spirited to a tightly secure location where he demonstrated his considerable psychic powers and where, ultimately, he encountered what seemed to be an intelligence operation surveilling the presence of extraterrestrials in our midst.

As Ingo's relationship with Axelrod deepened and he became accustomed to the intricate rituals of their communication, Axelrod himself took over the role of tasker, sending Ingo to locations of his choosing and asking him to file reports of his perceptions. One of those locations, Ingo writes, was the moon. But what he saw there on the lunar surface, made him not only question whether he had even traveled to the moon, but whether this unit of the United States government was sitting on a secret of such devastating importance, that it implied there was another reality which, if revealed, would change everything about the way we lived or thought about ourselves. This was, if true, a startling reality.

It began with a trip to the lunar surface. Ingo explained that he was able to project himself in the direction of the sun and then veer off toward the moon. When he believed he got there, he thought he'd landed somewhere else because of the strange anomalies he found. He saw something that looked like a road—something that two of our Apollo astronauts also said they saw—and even something that looked like, in Ingo's words, a geodesic "prefab structure" that Buckminster Fuller might have put up. The sights of structures and other artificial-looking constructs made Ingo doubt at first that he was on the moon. He asked Axelrod whether he had been given the correct coordinates. He questioned the entire process, wanted to break away, and even questioned what Axelrod and this special intelligence unit were up to. Finally he was convinced that this was not a game and Axelrod was straightforward about what he wanted Ingo Swann to do.

Back to the moon. Ingo again psychically navigated toward the sun and then veered off in the direction of the moon, following Axelrod's coordinates to the dark side of the surface. Of course, that's where any structures would be. Because the moon keeps the same face toward the earth at all times, anyone wanting to hide activity on the moon's surface would make sure to keep it on the side away from the earth. Ingo again perceived structures, what looked like roads, and even colored lights moving inside the craters. As he related his impressions to Axelrod, his analysis slipping into the raw reports and raising doubts in his mind even as he spoke, he fended off questions from Axelrod. He had asked the government agent not to speak to him during his narration. He said that questioning or comments of any kind could influence the way he was relating the data by suggesting to him ways that he would report. But Axelrod was insistent in his probing.

Finally, as he allowed Axelrod to comment, Ingo picked up on an impression that he was getting from Axelrod. Axelrod's questions were too pointed, too knowing. Axelrod wasn't sharing in the surprise that Ingo himself was feeling. After all, here he was on the moon and he was talking about structures that could not possibly have been natural. He was talking about buildings and domes, not just oddly shaped rocks. But through it all, Axelrod was almost cross-examining him, trying to focus him on the details. Almost in desperation, Ingo had to ask him whether what he was reporting on was even a surprise to Axelrod. He confronted him. "You knew this all along," he said. And Axelrod 'fessed up. They had suspected it. They had believed just what Ingo was telling them, and believed it for a long time. Of course they didn't have the facts or the ability to observe these objects on the lunar surface in any detail. But they knew they were there. Ingo brought out in greater detail what they thought they had observed from lunar orbiters.

Veritas promptus est!

Whatever this intelligence operation was, our government, or some secret bureau within it, absolutely *knew* that there was some form of artificial structure on the moon, not our home-built structures and not necessarily structures fabricated by the Russians. Besides, Axelrod told Ingo Swann, the United States didn't have any launch vehicles large enough or powerful enough to lift that amount of weight off the earth's surface. Neither did the Russians. It did not come from here.

There was no thought of his breaking away now, not when Ingo had it revealed to him that our government knew there was some kind of presence on the moon. But what kind of presence? Was this a long-dead civilization? Was it an abandoned outpost of an alien race but preserved there for millions of years? Was this proof that Zacharia Sitchen was right about Planet X and the moon? Ingo had to find these things out.

This time, encouraged by Axelrod, Ingo explored a whole range of lunar structures. He saw towers, bridges that seemed, x in his words, "to go nowhere," roads, and even different types of what he described as "houses," although he had no idea who could have lived there. What he saw was nothing less than an entire city, like an industrial park with types of "machinery" he'd never seen before. They were in and along the sides of craters, types of earth-moving equipment or tractors, they appeared to be, but what were they moving? They also seemed to be alongside factory-like structures. Dare he enter one of the structures?

In his book, *Penetration,* Ingo described something that looked to him like a "net" stretched over a crater. Time for a remote-viewing look-see. Ingo, in his own words, says, "I saw some kind of people busy at work on something I could not figure out. The place was dark. The 'air' was filled with a fine dust, and there was some kind of illumination—like a dark lime-green fog or mist" (*Penetration,* p. 57). Who were they? What were they?

They were humanlike, Swann writes. They looked like they were working, "digging into a hillside or a cliff," all of them males, and all of them absolutely naked. Ingo related his impressions to Axelrod who now seemed absolutely focused on every word Ingo said. As he spoke, he posed rhetorical questions, almost to guide his own navigation into the structure in the crater and almost to guide Axelrod's thinking. Then, all of a sudden, while Ingo was watching what his analytical mind would later call a "mining operation" take place, the psychic chemistry of the remote-viewing process changed dramatically.

Two of the humanoid figures amid the group he was watching, who were oblivious to being observed at first, suddenly became very animated and excited. They gestured to each other, began talking to each other, and suddenly "pointed" in Ingo's direction. If Ingo had believed himself to be invisible, he knew he was not the instant two of the entities he was observing suddenly looked directly at him. Busted!

When Ingo's fear at having been discovered, or worse, overwhelmed him, his reaction was flight. And with that sensation, the image before him began to fade. He was still in communication with Axelrod at that point, telling him that they spotted him. Axelrod, in the calmest possible voice, directed him to leave the lunar surface immediately. But there was something in Axelrod's voice, Ingo revealed, something below the surface that told him that whatever had happened up there, Axelrod not only knew the creatures he would encounter but knew that they had the ability to perceive Ingo's presence.

It's not that they saw him, Ingo would write about his ensuing conversation with Axelrod. It was almost as if there was a psychic fabric along the highway Ingo was traveling, a very thin membrane that linked the target and the viewer for that particular session. End the session and the fabric disappeared.

However, in this particular case, the humanoids on the moon, extraterrestrial or extradimensional or both, were conscious through their own telepathic grid of the psychic membrane that held Ingo. Thus, when something disturbed whatever frequency within which these creatures were existing, maybe by disrupting the telepathic envelope that surrounded them, the creatures were aware not only that something was there but where the disturbance was taking place. Reminiscent of Obi Wan's comment in *Star Wars* that there was a "disturbance" in the Force, this disturbance in the psychic chi of the humanoid's environment was probably as real and as palpable an appearance as if they were actually able to see Ingo on an earthly three-dimensional plane. I liken this to a story I heard years ago during the war in Kosovo about ways a potential enemy might pinpoint the location of a Stealth fighter or bomber. Maybe it was just urban myth, but it's applicable here. Imagine an area thick with cell phone and wireless service. Wireless signals are beamed down to cell phone relays and other wireless relays from satellites. If you could see the cell phone signal waves, you would see a fabric of signals from individual phone users to relays to a satellite almost like a web. What if you could translate that web of signals into a visual computer image? What if at that point, any object interrupting that image displayed an outline? What if that object were a Stealth aircraft? In that instance, even though radar might not be able to get a reading from the aircraft, a cell phone signal image enhancer might get a reverse image of the craft.

Therefore, in much the same way, I would surmise, the telepathic membrane that connected all of the creatures inside the lunar factory was disrupted by something with a different resonance that radiated a presence if not a shape. That disruption was the psychic projection of Ingo Swann who was perceiving these creatures. He spotted them. They spotted him and, by his presence, knew they were being observed. Question: When Ingo terminated the viewing session did he also cover up his psychic trail? In the alternative, did Ingo leave a psychic trail for telepathic tracking dogs to follow? Was Ingo's lunar-encounter with the humanoids, who'd become aware of his presence, a journey along a psychic superhighway traveled not just by the occasional remote viewer but by a whole host of interdimensionally enabled beings? Not even Axelrod could assure him that this did not happen.

Ingo's experiences, which eventually led him back to Los Angeles and back to a conversation with my Aunt Shafica Karagulla, did not end with his exit from that lunar session. He reveals in *Penetration* that while in an L.A. grocery market, he actually saw what he instinctively knew was an extraterrestrial, albeit in a human guise, shopping in the produce aisle. He was yanked from what might have been a very fateful encounter with this ET by Axelrod's agents who, themselves, were keeping the entity under surveillance. That made it blindingly clear to Ingo Swann that this group was not just investigating the existence of extraterrestrials and what their intentions might be, if they existed, but they were absolutely certain of their existence and were something akin to a counterintelligence force surveilling ETs who were already on earth. And Ingo Swann, whose psychic abilities and research into remote viewing at the Stanford Research Institute made him uniquely qualified to conduct surveillance operations, was right in the thick of it. How much more intense would this get?

In subsequent chapters of *Penetration*, Ingo tells the story of how Axelrod and his agents accompanied Ingo to a remote site in Alaska where he was privy not only to the touchdown of what was described as an extraterrestrial space craft, he was actually fired on by that craft with some kind of vaporizing ray that torched parts of the thick underbrush where Axelrod and Ingo were hiding. There were aliens living on earth and aliens in space ships attacking what they sensed were human ob-servers. It was a scene right out of *War of the Worlds*.

We read all about this in *Penetration,* but these are Ingo Swann's impressions told entirely from his point of view. They point to a fantastic reality and, even taken at face value, they more than suggest that things are not what they seem. They do lead one to ask, however, whether there is any corroboration to anything Ingo Swann claims to have seen. Axelrod, as one would believe, has since faded away, probably assuming a new name and new identity in another part of the U.S. intelligence forest. But did anyone see what Ingo said he saw on the moon?

Corroboration can come from strange places. In *Penetration,* Ingo writes that when he reviewed his own sketches of what he saw, the bridges, roadways, arches, and domelike structures, they reminded him of the drawings George Leonard made of his observations of lunar anomalies that appeared in his book, *Somebody Else Is on the Moon.*

In addition to the George Leonard book, Ingo's impressions of structures on the lunar surface are also corroborated by NASA's own R-277 report of 500 years of anomalous lunar activity. This report, compiled by NASA in advance of the Apollo missions, documents observations made by individuals, both amateur and professional, in which they describe strange events taking place on or above the lunar surface. The Elizabethan poet and playwright Christopher Marlowe, for example, described lights hovering above the moon and a strange mist around certain craters. Colonial New England fire-and-brimstone preacher Cotton Mather also described strange lights around the moon. There were similar observations by the English Royal Observatory in the nineteenth century. And a New York newspaper reporter in the 1940s also reported that he saw actual structures on the moon that looked to him like bridges and roadways. Ingo Swann's reports of structures, roadways, arches leading nowhere, and even bridges, certainly comports with some of the observations in NASA's own unclassified report, which is available to anyone at the NASA website and has been cited in UFO publications and in the *UFO Magazine UFO Encyclopedia*.

Another form of corroboration, of sorts, came from Army remote viewer and author of the Army's CRV manual, Paul H. Smith, who, in interviews with us, revealed that Ingo Swann had given him lunar coordinates as part of his training. Smith explained that his sketches based on his impressions were similar to Ingo Swann's and that Smith, too, had seen things ostensibly on the lunar surface that seemed weird and out of place. However, in sharing notes with Harold Puthoff, one of the original remote-viewing researchers and managers, Smith said that part of what he had seen on the moon might well have been reflections of what was in Ingo Swann's mind from his remote viewing sessions. Smith explained to us that it's not impossible for the impressions in the tasker's mind to be transferred to the viewer's mind so that during a session, the remote viewer actually picks up a signal not to the target directly but to the target as a reflection of what the tasker either has seen, expects to see, or even hopes to see. This might have been the case, Smith says, when he visited the places that Swann saw and picked up on images similar to what Swann sketched out.

Thus, the images Smith saw might have been residual images in Swann's mind that were overlaid on what Smith saw when given the lunar coordinates.

With that as a caveat, however, Paul H. Smith still believes that he saw something on the moon that he cannot explain away as an aberration. Whether there are actual ETs walking around on earth and whether the individual who introduced himself to Swann as Axelrod was truly working for the U.S. intelligence services or the military are not the issues. What is the issue, Smith said, is that he saw things on the moon which, if they were not overlays from Ingo Swann's own mind, should not have been there if the NASA party line that Americans have been given over the past forty plus years is to be believed. Maybe what Ingo Swann and Paul Smith perceived were also a form of confirmation of what Richard Hoagland has been telling me on the air for years and what Zacharia Sitchen has predicted we would find someday, that another civilization had visited the Moon as well as Mars.

But even that's not the most important thing that came out of the Ingo Swann book and Paul Smith interviews. The blockbuster, from our perspective, is that all of the Ingo Swann observations and the later observations that were made by Paul Smith were the result of psychic viewing, remote viewing, a form of psychic teleportation to a different place and possibly even a different dimension. This was an activity that according to the traditional laws of physics as most of us were given to understand them in high school and college, and what we believe we know about our own physical mental abilities, should not exist. People who have a sixth sense or who are telepathically gifted are somehow different from the rest of us. We are taught to fear them. The Pilgrim settlers in the New England colonies burned these kind of people at the stake as witches. Joan of Arc, who claimed to have heard voices from God, was also burned at the stake. Edgar Cayce, who, according to Joel Martin and William J. Birnes in *The Haunting of the Presidents,* practically ran the Woodrow Wilson White House after the president was incapacitated by illness and who claimed the ability to cure people via remote viewing, is still considered some sort of fringe New Age figure despite the absolute documentation of his abilities. In other words, the very type of activity that a mainstream military officer like Major Paul Smith talks about is considered off the chart by most people even though, in Ingo Swann's own words, "the proof of its existence is the fact that it works."

Before answering the question, What does all this say, the Ingo Swann story continues.

Back in Los Angeles and actually before having successfully been rescued from two encounters with extraterrestrials—one in a Hollywood supermarket and the other in Alaska—by Axelrod and company, Ingo decided to pay a visit to my aunt, Dr. Shafica Karagulla, a straight-up lab-coat clad neuropsychiatrist, who had studied the claims and stories of Edgar Cayce. Dr. Karagulla had also conducted her own research into psychic phenomena and, by the time her old friend Ingo Swann called on her, had become the center of a group of free thinkers and experimental psychologists in Los Angeles. If the celebrated Madame Blavatsky could have been reincarnated in early 1970s Los Angeles, she might well have been my Aunt Shafica.

But, according to Ingo, Shafica was at one time even more plugged in than Madame Blavatsky. With her experience in neuropsychology and her experiments with higher sense perception outside of the mainstream of medical practice, Shafica was well aware of the potential of human extrasensory experience. Ingo suggested that because of Shafica's relationships with Middle Eastern thinkers, she had had additional experience with U.S. Intelligence agencies and thus might have known about the very things that Ingo himself had learned from dealing with Axelrod and company.

At dinner with Dr. Karagulla and her companion and assistant Viola Neal, Ingo asked Shafica's opinion about extraterrestrials on earth, strange goings-on on the moon, interplanetary aliens and our government's knowledge of them.

"Of course," my aunt replied, her deep background in research on the abilities of human beings to view events on earth from a much higher plane than most of us experience enabling her to answer with such certainty. "They're here. We know about them. The government knows about them."

SHAFICA KARAGULLA AND HIGHER-SENSORY PERCEPTION

W hat did Dr. Shafica Karagulla know and why did Ingo Swann make it a point to talk to her when he found out that our government knew about extraterrestrial life forms on earth and about their ability to recognize those who were remote-viewing them?

That is, in essence what my caller from Canada is asking about.

"I read *Penetration,*" the caller says. "At first I didn't believe more than half of it, but when Swann said that he went to Shafica and I read her book, I knew there was something to it."

And indeed there was. It turns out that my aunt Shafica knew a lot. First, she had worked for U.S. intelligence way back when. She was a specialist on the Middle East. But, most important, she had conducted scientific research into the very things Ingo was asking her about and had made some startling discoveries.

Who was Dr. Shafica Karagulla? She was a traditional neurologist and psychiatrist, a medical doctor whose clinical practice involved treating patients with severely debilitating conditions such as grand mal epilepsy, violent hallucinations, and other mental illnesses that normally required institutionalization. She specialized in the neurological side of psychiatric research, examining the kinds of symptoms that often caused physical brain damage to patients. Moreover, simply as a scientist, Shafica was fascinated by the operation of the human brain, the functionality and adaptability of the human mind to reconfigure itself to changing circumstances, and its ability to heal. She was a dedicated physician and a clinician who was not afraid of engaging in outside-the-box thinking and research. If someone were suffering from neurological scar tissue, a lesion on the brain, Dr. Karagulla was the kind of doctor who desperately wanted to know what kinds of psychological and emotional symptoms resulted from that lesion. She was of a generation of doctors who had inherited from their early-twentieth-century medical school professors a ready eagerness to engage in surgeries and shock treatments for psychological symptoms, and she was not happy about the heavy-handedness of those kinds of procedures.

And Shafica was also to a large degree responsible for my fascination with all things paranormal.

In her book, *Breakthrough to Creativity,* one of the anthemic books of the New Age, especially in California, Shafica documents her journey from traditional psychiatry to an investigation and ultimately an embrace of a form of human spirituality that at the time might have been considered New Age but now is almost an accepted part of workbench science. Of course, it was workbench science even during Shafica's time for those who were trying to reverse-engineer remote viewing so as to make it fiscally palatable for the budget-conscious financial overseers of the Army's expenditures. Who knows whether Shafica knew that because she was approaching the art from a different discipline even though she told Ingo Swann she had worked for the American clandestine services.

What was the event that triggered Shafica's interest in what she described as a higher-sensory perception? Perhaps it was her visit to Dr. Wilder Penfield's clinic in Montreal where she observed his experiments with patients suffering from severe forms of epilepsy. Back in the 1950s, before the advent of to-day's psychotropic pharmaceuticals, the treatment of severe forms of epilepsy was limited. And at a time before CAT scans and ultrasound diagnostics, we didn't know what was going on across the neurological pathways of a patient's cerebral cortex while the patient was experiencing symptoms. What we knew, we knew too many times from attempts at corrective surgeries and, in the worse cases, postmortem surgeries.

Often, grand mal seizures threatened to cause permanent physiological damage to the neural circuitry in the brain because of the surges of electricity from hemisphere to hemisphere. As a result, there were often radical forms of surgery indicated by doctors, which, unfortunately, sometimes left the patients in a diminished neurological condition. But it was the state of the medical art at the time.

Also, persons suffering from severe forms of clinical depression, conditions so debilitating that the sufferers could not even get out of bed and take care of their own personal hygiene, were left with few options. Now, of course, there are mood-altering drugs and less dramatic types of surgery. But back then doctors often prescribed extensive series of electro-convulsive therapy—shock treatment—to jolt a patient out of life-threatening depression. My aunt Shafica was one of those neuropsychiatrists looking for a lighter therapeutic hand in dealing with these patients.

Her research led her to discover the work that Wilder Penfield was doing up in Canada with patients who were suffering from lesions on the brain. Dr. Penfield was treating other types of neurological impairments and illnesses as well. Penfield reported that in ascertaining the extent of lesion damage, often the result of repeated epileptic seizures, he stimulated parts of a patient's cerebral cortex with very low voltage so as to measure the neurological response in that area. Were the nerves alive or dead? To his surprise, many of his patients, who were fully awake during this procedure, spontaneously responded with reports of memories they had long since forgotten. Not only were the circuits alive, they had stored events long forgotten by their conscious minds. But it was much, much more than memory.

These patients, according to Dr. Penfield, responded not as if they were recalling simple memories, but acting as if they were actually there reliving their memories. They not only experienced the sights, but heard the sounds of the events as they resonated in their brains, tasted the tastes, and reacted to the olfactory stimulation as if the smells themselves were permeating the room. In other words, in their minds, the patients were actually, physically present sometimes across decades in time, locked within a living hallucination of a past event.

Penfield was astonished at his patients' respective degrees of recall, the minute details they were able to report, and the ability to report as if they were actually there at a different point in time. It was a phenomenon not unlike Ingo Swann's description of being inside one of the lunar structures while he was reporting to Axelrod on what he was perceiving. Penfield's patients reported they were in the past, sometimes as little children, speaking to parents or siblings, experiencing the feelings they had at that time not as memories but as real, visceral, emotions, and experiencing the physical sensations as well.

Penfield's research into the multiphasic nature of human experience, the ability of the brain to function in the present while feeding itself with vivid experiences from alternate realities, helped form part of the physiological basis for what became known as transactional analysis in the 1970s. Specifically, in *I'm OK, You're OK* by Thomas Harris, the author refers to Penfield's experiments as a kind of proof that one's psychological child coexists within one's personality and influences, often dramatically, the way the person reacts to life's situations by writing scripts that a person constantly acts out in transactions with others. But Aunt Shafica was not pursuing research into transactional analysis when she came on Penfield's work. It was her fascination with the dualistic experience that patients reported to Penfield that inspired her to travel to Montreal to become a part of Dr. Penfield's research.

In Montreal, Shafica writes, she saw firsthand how patients reacted to cortical stimulation by reliving specific incidents in their past. These experiencers were aware of where they were, that they were on an operating table in a hospital in the presence of a neurosurgeon, and that they were reporting their impressions to him. Yet, at the same time they were in another place, in another time, and were literally hearing the voices of people long dead. Were they hallucinating? That's what Dr. Penfield believed. He theorized that since all of one's memories are stored somewhere in the cerebral tissue, the stimulation of a certain spot with a low-voltage current could replay those memories as if replaying a videotape. In other words, we never fully forget, and our memories are always churning somewhere in our brains.

But Shafica Karagulla was struck by something else. She didn't necessarily see these patients as hallucinating as much as actually experiencing events on a higher order of perception. Their recall was too specific. They were simultaneously engaged in conversations with Penfield as well as with people in their vision. Mentally, if not physically, they were inhabiting more than one place at one time. This was a phenomenon she had not seen before outside of those suffering from psychotic hallucinations or out-and-out hallucinatory schizophrenics talking and gesturing to imaginary demons or other tormentors, or even claiming to have heard the voice of spirits or angels, and it inspired her to research this further.

Shafica writes that she was so impressed with the possibilities of human experience that Penfield's experiments suggested, that she expanded her research into other areas of alternate perception. And that led to her discovery of the work of Edgar Cayce, the "Sleeping Prophet," who had died in 1945. Shafica said that what fascinated her most about Cayce were his descriptions of how he left his body to view distant events, events in the future, and telepathically visit individuals with various illnesses, which he was able to diagnose. Shafica pored over the records of Cayce's activities and spoke to people who knew and worked with him. She was a skeptic, a scientist, who wanted proof of some of the incredible claims that Cayce's followers made.

Was this man able to see the future? Was he able to astral-project himself to distant locations? Was he able to effect cures in those who sought his help because of his ability to perceive things that traditional medical doctors failed to see? What was the methodology that Cayce employed to effect his miracle cures?

Part of Cayce's process was to induce a form of self-hypnosis, not sleep as we understand it, but a kind of zoning out in which, his followers claimed, he was able to perceive not only the person who was suffering from some undiagnosable ailment, but the person's past lives as well. In Dr. Kenzo Yamamoto's recently published *Unified Theory of the Cosmos,* a book critical of Cayce's career, he quotes psychologist Gina Cerminara's research into Cayce in *Many Mansions* for her argument that seemed to agree with Shafica Karagulla's. Both Dr. Cerminara and Dr. Karagulla agree that part of the importance of Cayce's achievements lies in the documentation of those claims by many reputable psychologists and the "credible accounts" of both his clairvoyant sessions and the cures he was able to perform. Almost as important, many of the records of Edgar Cayce's activities were recorded, and became available to anyone wanting to study him. In the sixty years since Cayce's death, numerous books have been written about his life and his work and, as Joel Martin and myself have written in the forthcoming *The Haunting of America,* (Forge, 2008) he has become one of America's most important twentieth-century prophets, perhaps, even, the most important clairvoyant in the country's history. Yet, Shafica wondered, what did Cayce actually see when he telepathically visited his patients?

Cayce was able to perceive his patients' past lives, pinpoint the aspects of those lives that seemed to have manifested themselves in the ailments of the persons' present lives, and described the causal relationship between what happened in previous lives, even lives lived out thousands of years earlier, and the present lives. Cases in point? Cerminara writes about Cayce's explanation to a woman who became a polio victim when she was in her mid-thirties and was left completely wheelchair-bound. When she asked Cayce about the cause of her affliction, he explained that she had been a member of Emperor Nero's court in ancient Rome and laughed when Christians were tortured in the public arenas and left crippled. Hence, their fate had become hers. It was karma.

There are those, Dr. Yamamoto among them, who will argue the morality of Cayce's visions. They will say that karma alone cannot be responsible for the fate of those in present lives because it denies the very basis of human existence: the ability to make moral choices. Are we bound in this life to suffer the sins we inflicted on those in former lives? Do we live out our lives under a moral sanction, an understanding of which, we hope, will lead us to less burdensome existences in our ensuing lives? If that's what some philosophies teach, so be it. But it was not what Shafica Karagulla was after in her research. What she saw was the ability of a human being to traverse time and dimension so as to project him- or herself telepathically to a different plane was the ability of all people to reach a higher-sensory perception. In other words, if Edgar Cayce could accomplish these feats, might there be others who could do the same? And if there were others, might this ability to engage in this form of projection be part of the human sensory set, inhibited over thousands of years of human civilization by religions fearing that level of individual power and by the disdain and sanctions from governments? Remember the Salem witch trials. Would you, if you were psychically gifted, have publicly displayed your abilities, foretold someone's fate, explained their afflictions in terms of acts performed in past lives? Not likely, because you would have been accused of witchcraft, tortured into confessing, and burned at the stake.

But it was the twentieth century, and Shafica Karagulla did not fear accusations of consort with the Devil. She was more concerned about derisive comments from members of her own medical profession, but she nevertheless intended to find a sound psychological and physiological basis for the ability of individuals to achieve a higher-sensory perceptivity (HSP).

Gathering her resources, Shafica cast a long net to find people who had experienced different forms of either telepathic communication or paranormal events. She also set out to interview paranormal researchers around the world. Because she was a scientist, my aunt wrote, she took no one at his or her word, but conducted her own tests. She made sure there were no other influences or ways her subjects could trick the observers. She combined confirmed anecdotal testimony from witnesses with actual tests of her subjects' ability to pick out cards hidden in a deck, symbols on cards, and the like to get some form of score. Next, she asked her highest-testing subjects to help her conduct research with other subjects. Then, when she went to Europe and back to the Middle East to interview researchers, she asked some of her subjects to accompany her.

The result of her years of research and experimentation into this form of communication and perception was an absolutely stunning accumulation of data, which constituted, she says, absolute proof that there was another kind of alternate mode of perception that was as scientifically confirmable as perception via the rest of a person's senses. In her writings, she is absolutely convinced that there is a higher-sensory perception, called by whatever name you want to call it, that constitutes exactly what Ingo Swann taught his remote-viewing students and what Swann himself says he practiced.

Driven by a desire to map out the ways the different higher-sensory perceptions manifest themselves in different people, whom she calls "Sensitives," Shafica Karagulla looked for all the different levels of perception her Sensitives enjoyed. For example, because she saw that low-voltage levels of current could stimulate the human brain when applied to different areas of the cerebral cortex, Shafica sought to find out if the brain or bodies of people also emanated levels of energy. Medical doctors know that living organisms generate electricity, but was this electricity also wireless? Were there energy flows around people that effect the ways other people perceive them? And could her Sensitives see or otherwise perceive these energy flows?

Shafica writes that she was thrilled to discover that not only could her Sensitives perceive orbits of energy waves around people, but that these waves actually radiated a color or colors, changed colors, and, in specific situations, mingled with or affected the energy waves of other people. In one stunning experiment, Shafica was able to catalog the ways stage performers engaged their audience. Her Sensitives saw that the lines of energy glowed and pulsated when a performer entered the stage. They saw that the lines of energy from the audience, although orbiting around individuals, seemed to merge to almost a group energy. Then, almost as if a correlation to the behavior of the performer who must engage his or her audience, bringing them into the dramatic conceit, the lines of energy from the performer expanded to encompass the entire audience. What a thrill it must have been for my aunt to hear her Sensitive's report of this phenomenon: engaging people are not just mysteriously so, there was actually a physical manifestation, perceived by an individual endowed with HSP, that demonstrated as scientifically as possible that what looked like a pure effect of personality was visually represented in a realm that most people not so endowed could not see.

Shafica Karagulla was transported by what her research had revealed. Imagine, she told her readers, someone in the nineteenth century suggesting that someday astronomers whose telescopes could not see distant stars would be able to listen to them because stars emanated invisible radio waves. At the time it would have been unthinkable to all but a few. Waves that people could not see but that revealed the existence of something physical? But, by the time she was researching human energy lines, Shafica Karagulla could point to radio telescopes as proof positive of part of her argument.

For me, reading *Breakthrough to Creativity* was an enlightening experience because it demonstrated through the correlation of anecdotal reports and documentation of human experimentation that there was a world of reality, which, though unseen, was perceivable through an alternate vision. And, even more important for my way of thinking, if one Sensitive could perceive that world, other people had the potential of being trained to perceive it. Ingo Swann, therefore, was correct when he said that some people might be better endowed with the ability to remote view than others, but it was a skill that was thoroughly trainable. Paul H. Smith, in his book, says that the training is like taking piano lessons. Only one in a hundred million might have the talent of a Mozart, but anyone can learn to plunk out a tune or navigate his or her way through a fake book so as to entertain a party in the basement playroom on an old upright piano.

The revelations Shafica enjoyed at her discovery of human energy lines and the way they seemed to react to changing situations and moods was but mere preparation to her subsequent discovery that Sensitives could perceive the energy waves emanated by certain crystals and gems. In a series of experiments, Shafica walked her subjects into museums where they reported on what they perceived when they looked at different types of crystals or gemstones. They talked about the waves arcing around diamonds and how they differed from those arcing around rubies or sapphires.

When her subjects held crystalline objects in their hands, they described how the colors of the waves seemed to change when they held them in their right versus left hands. When they changed their direction of perception, sensitive subjects also reported on subtle changes in the way the waves were manifested. Did this mean, Dr. Karagulla asked, that crystals and gems were not simply dead objects emitting certain energies, but almost living, attuning themselves to latitudinal or longitudinal energy lines? What if, I thought as I read her book, there is a kind of nexus of energy wave lines defined by the earth's magnetic field as it interacts with a variety of gems, crystals, plant life, and animal life? I believed that my aunt had demonstrated, or at least discovered, one piece of the puzzle that helped to define the meaning of Gaia, the living planet earth.

In other parts of her research, Shafica discovered that certain types of photography could be affected by human energy and that there were photographic investigators who had actually photographed different types of energy waves. She also sought to define the nature of her Sensitives, explaining that many individuals endowed with higher-sensory perceptivity chose to keep their gifts a secret. After all, being able to pick up on another person's energy field, "psychometrize" another person through the energy expressed in that person's handwriting, read other people's minds or emotions simply by receiving telepathic energy waves, and otherwise demonstrate an ability to see what others cannot was a dangerous game. Such practices in the Middle Ages amounted to charges of heresy and witchcraft. And the Bible, as Joel Martin aptly points out in *The*

Haunting of the Presidents, states specifically, "thou shalt not suffer a witch to live."

Therefore, when Shafica demonstrated that higher-sense perceptivity wasn't witchcraft or anything supernatural at all, but only a manifestation of a power of perception that's probably some part of all our genetic makeup, she was writing powerful stuff.

Throughout most of her book, Shafica Karagulla methodically documents, first, her discovery of the possibility of a higher-sensory perception of an alternate reality, and then her rigorous scientific experimentation to compile verifiable evidence as to the way this form of perception manifests itself in individuals. She is not a spiritual guru, not a self-described prophet or a true-believer touchy-feely type advocate of human spiritual potential. She does not seek to proselytize, although the group of believers that eventually assembled around her did proselytize to some extent. Dr. Karagulla was a scientist who discovered that human beings do have a whole other way of perceiving reality such that the definition of reality itself might need some adjustment if not outright expansion. She talks about those HSP-endowed individuals in history who, perhaps unwittingly, were able to harness their HSP gifts to enable to see what others couldn't, predict outcomes whose potentials eluded most people, and sustain themselves in times of difficulty.

She points specifically to George Washington's vision at Valley Forge, a time of desperation for the beleaguered Continental Army wintering outside the British-occupied Philadelphia. In his darkest moments of self-doubt, while looking at his ravaged troops, beset by disease and in the deep freeze of an icebound Northeast winter, General Washington perceived the image of what might be described as a heavenly being, an angel who predicted the future. It was a vision the poet William Blake vision might have created, to be sure, but it was documented in Washington's conversations with his aides. It was a vision in which the angelic being described to the forlorn leader of the tattered revolutionary army a history of what would become of the Union, the United States of America, in which the army would weather this terrible winter, and then endure three subsequent challenges to its very existence. In the final challenge, perhaps yet to be experienced, the entire world would turn against the United States, but, divinely ordained, the Union would ultimately triumph and endure. This a vision described not only in *Breakthrough to Creativity,* but also in great detail by Joel Martin and William J. Birnes in *The Haunting of the Presidents.*

What Shafica Karagulla demonstrated, first by experimental research, and then by anecdotal documentation, was that HSP was not something new, but something very old. It was a way to tap into a reality that existed perhaps beyond the realm of the five senses but certainly within the realm of human perception. It was a world that seemed to be composed of multiple realities that intersected with each other like railroad switch tracks and allowed those who could perceive those tracks to change direction so as to avoid disaster. But for my mind, as I pursued my own research into the scientific background of what happened to me that day I floated to the ceiling, Shafica Karagulla demonstrated that I wasn't crazy or hallucinating. There was another reality in which human beings could navigate and within which, if you had the appropriate training and took the proper precautions, you could journey not only in space, but through time.

6

The Psychic Superhighway, Shamanism, and the Power of Dreams

I 'm talking about remote viewing tonight as the beginning of a story about human empowerment and how science itself has shown that there is a reality out there that most people never touch or see deliberately. This is a reality that touches our lives and, if we can only be shown how to navigate within it or through it, we will reach an unlimited potential. Our government knows all about this reality, in part, because of the Army's remote-viewing program.

As Paul H. Smith revealed in his interviews with us, the Army, in order to secure the budgetary allocations necessary to fund its remote-viewing Stargate program, found that rather than describe the events as purely psychic or telepathic in origin, they had to be purely physical in origin. There could be no New Age, no human spirituality, nothing of the sort. There had to be workbench, reproducible, hard science grounded on a physical explanation of the events the Army was trying to explain. In so doing, the theorists Ingo Swann and Dr. Hal Puthoff, laid out a fortuitous path from exigencies of military budgeting back through the twentieth-century quantum physicists, to turn-of-the-twentieth-century Vienna and the emerging human consciousness theories of the *fin-de-siècle* science of psychology.

These psychology theories presupposed, as Wilder Penfield would later confirm with hard physical, quantifiable evidence, that the experiences of individual human beings were not evanescent memories that simply faded away over time, ultimately losing all impact of reality. They were stored somewhere, in another part of the mind like data on a disk drive, where they would continue to pump, just like underground machines, the emotions associated with them—emotions that affected just about every aspect of a person's personality to some degree. We are, in no small measure, the results of our experiences, as well as the result of our genetic makeup. But the larger part of these experiences, like huge menacing icebergs on a moonless North Atlantic night, move about in an area below the level of our conscious awareness informing how we react to people, things, events, and the daily frustrations of life. The sum total of our subconscious experiences form a filter, a prism, or even a translation mechanism that structures how we interpret what we see.

Whereas Sigmund Freud and his associates hypothesized this world of the subconscious as something that could be talked about and even observed through the behavior of others, Wilder Penfield actually touched it when he stimulated areas of a patient's cerebral cortex with a low-voltage current. That stimulation awakened within the patient not just memories, but proof that an individual's experiences don't simply disappear or fade away, they are folded away amid the millions of convolutions in the gray matter of the brain where at least most of our consciousness resides. All experiences exist simultaneously within our brain, Penfield discovered, defying a conscious chronological overlay that pigeonholes events into distant past, past, recent past, and present. It was, Penfield found, a physiological correlative to what Freud and his associates had postulated forty years earlier.

One of those associates, who later broke with Professor

Freud, was Swiss psychologist Carl Gustav Jung, who soon became a famous researcher in his own right and the founder of a movement that would inform the writings of the comparative cultural mythology scholar Joseph Campbell and even influence modern ufology. For our purposes, Jungian psychology, with its emphasis on a shared reservoir of human thought in which an individual's unconscious mind partakes from an archetypal pool of shapes and symbols representing shared deeper meanings of human existence, was an important approach for understanding the human mind.

Also for our purposes, the mind's relationship to a larger symbolic reality, which held as much significance in defining the matrix within which human beings navigate and deal with one another, was as much to say that people had the ability to remote view on a daily basis even if to a lesser extent than the professional remote-viewers trained by the military. Thus— and this is a very simplistic comparison—while dream interpretations for Freud are manifestations of the outcropping of memories buried in the subconscious, they were insights into an *individual's* reservoir of stored knowledge. For Dr. Jung, dream interpretation could mean tapping into a *collective* reservoir of human experience. The individual, in a Jungian psychological universe, opened up a link to a storehouse of symbolic information shared by others. This link implied that the dreamer was psychically journeying to and retrieving pertinent information from this universal collective of information. This was almost like a computer terminal's retrieving information from a database of all reality: past, present, and future, and generated in a special language of symbols.

In the Jungian paradigm of reality, a person's dream state, during which the actual analytical overlay of waking life is by definition shut down, the person is actually capable of communication with the collective unconscious of the entire species in a way similar to the type of communication posited by Ingo Swann and Hal Puthoff when they presupposed a database of all information as the place where remote viewers gather their information. In this way, not only are ordinary or untrained people able to communicate with this vast database, but the very act of dreaming puts the individual in a state where such communication is possible.

Now for the exciting stuff.

Jung went beyond the dream state in his description of how the individual can connect with the collective unconscious of all humanity. Jung suggested that dreams were only an aspect of connecting with a great link. Dreams tapped into the switchboard the individual uses to connect to the database, but they were only a preliminary step to a true unity with what I like to describe as a great link. A person, any person, Jung suggested, could train him- or herself to override or even shed one's ego, so as to become kind of a superself. In this way, one can extend his or her individual consciousness beyond the constraints of "I" into a form of communication with a universe where all things that were ever dreamed of or conceived still exist. One could, as later experiments would point out, by diminishing his or her self-awareness, actually influence the way the future would unfold. This process, this greater individualization, although not conceived of the way the remote viewers were trained, was nevertheless Jung's description of how to achieve the same goal.

Jung's model actually works. Although it was a theory based on the descriptions of those people, from classical times to the nineteenth century and from the shamans of indigenous peoples to the psychics who populated the late nineteenth century's "Great Age of Spiritualism," the model coincides almost point for point with what Ingo Swann and Hal Puthoff taught the remote viewer trainees. They taught their trainees to tune out their perceptions of the real world, to shut off their labeling and categorization mechanism that they use to define what they see, and, thus, allow themselves to see only raw data. As whacky or as nonsensical as their perceptions were, that's what they were told to write down. No analysis allowed here. Only raw data impressions were to be captured on paper. In this way, whatever was perceived was recorded without any coloring.

When you look at what Ingo's training was supposed to accomplish, you can see that it was very close to what Jung described as the squelching of the ego—the "I"—that kept individuals separate from one another—so as to allow the perceiver to join the reservoir of the collective unconscious.

Do remote viewers travel to the collective unconscious?

In a real sense, they do. And what's important is that the scientific explanation Ingo Swann and Hal Puthoff used to legitimatize the science of remote viewing presupposes the existence of something very close to the Jungian collective unconscious. They did this for the very practical reason of gaining funding for their experiments from the government. You see, the government doesn't fund psychic, New Age, or hippie stuff. They want science. Tell a senator that he or she is being asked to put up millions of dollars for something New Age and you'll get a resounding no. Tell that senator that there is actual, reproducible, quantifiable science behind it and you may get a yes. So Ingo Swann and Hal Puthoff set out to explain that science to the bean counters inside the Beltway.

They did so by creating a valid explanation for how remote

viewing worked. When Ingo and Hal theorized that there had to exist a matrix of all things living and nonliving, timeless and complete, infinite yet palpable, they posited that remote viewers didn't mentalistically go to the location they were viewing, they picked up their perceptions of that location from this matrix. Similarly, when Jung theorized the nature of the abilities of the shamans of indigenous peoples and prophets of ancient times, he presupposed that they were able to accomplish what Swann and Puthoff taught their trainees, a shutting off of the sense of self so as to allow impressions to flood in.

Both prophets and medicine men and the remote viewers shared the capacity to partake of a great link of all human existence and experience and in so doing be in all places at once, be present at all times at once, and move across a multiplicity of universes of all possibilities. This was an existence, which, in Jung's world, was partly informed by superarchetypes of images. Thus, human beings from different cultures and different experiences shared the same types of visions and probably understood the same kinds of myths. In Ingo's theory, this was perhaps more like the world of forms that Plato described, forms that imparted meaning to objects on earth. Regardless of whose theory you chose, however, both theories presupposed a nexus of shared human consciousness from which psychic travelers could partake and in which they could participate across all boundaries of distance and time.

The process of this communication was the same as well, requiring the sublimation of one part of one's self, one's critical or analytical self, so that another aspect of the traveler's mind could freely perceive what was in the matrix. The analytical aspect of one's mind interfered with the influx of raw data, naming it, categorizing it, and commenting on the likelihood of its existence. Rather than accepting what was perceived, a person's sense of self acted like a prism or sluice gate created out of the sum total of one's experiences through which the raw perception was filtered. This made accurate perception impossible because a person's ego almost always determines one's ability to perceive.

Think of this in a real-world situation in which someone at work tells you a joke that he might find funny or benign, but which causes you to take offense. You make judgments every day about things—which are good and bad or threatening and nonthreatening. In reality, these very same things may be neither. They may only be things in and of themselves with no emotional or moral value until you apply the emotional or analytical qualifications. Doesn't Zen teach us to weigh each event equally, treating it as something that is rather than filtering it through our categorization process? When we assign values to what we perceive, we lessen the value of what is perceived and increase the value of our filtering system because we see what we want to see more often than seeing what is.

Of course, only a fool would counsel someone not to realize that a speeding car approaching you in an intersection signals danger or that a snarling dog behind a fence has its own issues that might not comport with yours. And you wouldn't rest your hand on a hot stove without thinking twice about it or stop prairie-dogging and duck back into your cubicle at work when the fault-finding and always short-tempered office manager is making the morning rounds. Your experience has taught you how to stay out of danger in the everyday world where you define things in terms of self-protection. However, what if you could learn to turn off your automatic self-categorization process just for the sake of experiencing something raw from an entirely different place?

In Eastern meditative religions, there is a process to achieve this higher or altered state of reality. In the many books written by Carlos Castaneda on the Yaqui Indian way of knowledge, the author's teacher, Don Juan, lays out another process, albeit more chemical than emotional. For Jung, this was a process of finding the superself, the larger ego that encompassed human existence, rather than tethering oneself to the smaller ego that defined the individual's sense of self. And in the coordinate remote-viewing program, Ingo Swann and Hal Puthoff taught their students how to train themselves to lay aside their analytical processes to enable them to report only what they perceived without naming the things or events.

Insofar as sleep is the turning off of the logical mind, it acts much the same way as sublimating the analytical mind and opening up one's mind to communication with the matrix of all things. This is why ancient philosophers, shamans of indigenous peoples, and modern spiritualists say that dreams are telepathic. Joseph predicted the seven years of plenty and seven years of famine from Pharaoh's dreams, both classical Greek and Roman literature are filled with interpretations of dream messages, and dream interpretation today is a thriving business. Freud based much of his therapy on the interpretation of dreams, as did Carl Jung. Dreams can be telepathic in that they allow the dreamer to interact with the psychic reservoir of human experience and bring back some insightful perception, even though the dreamer may not be able to understand it or reject it outright.

In this way, all of us, at the very least through our dream

states, are telepathic and capable of communicating with the matrix of all things. Some people are more psychic than others and perhaps some people are more in touch with their innate psychic abilities than others. But even if it's limited to a dream state, not only is each individual capable of making a psychic connection, each individual is aware to some extend of his or her own psychic potential. That is scary to many people because a dream is the opening of a doorway into a place not governed by the physical rules of our universe. Dreams tell us that there are more things out there than just what we see, hear, and smell. Dreams also tell us that people we believe are dead are still very much alive and in touch with what's going on in our own minds.

There are those psychologists who will tell us that dreams are simply manifestations of what is going on in our own minds. Dreams are the byproduct of the brain's need to store memories, to find locations for specific memories, burying some so as to protect the conscious mind from their unpleasantness or pain, calling up others because events in waking life have triggered something down deep in memory. But, how many of us, on waking up from a particularly vivid dream have said, in the lingering moments when we are still seized by the dream's poignancy, "This was no dream"? How many of us have felt that what we begin to tuck away neatly in our logical mind was not just a routine aberration of sleep, but actually a step into another reality where we also live and belong.

Dreams give us messages. People in dreams haunt us and tell us things we can only appreciate in dreams. In dreams there is no past and no future, only the immediate present. We move freely from our childhood to our adulthood without any discordancy as our childhood selves bump into our adult selves.

Our dreams can be three-dimensional, providing us with a belief of memories of events that may or may not have ever existed in our waking lives. In dreams we accept the dead as living and give them credence. In dreams we live in a telepathic universe in which we have the power to fly, to walk on water, to talk with spirits, to travel in time, and to travel out of our bodies so as to take on the physical embodiment of someone else and look at ourselves from the outside. In these ways, dreams have their own logic and power.

If we can fly in dreams, float in dreams, and move instantly from one place to another in dreams, we should realize that in dreams we are beings with superpowers. We can jump as high as the former Chicago Bulls superhero Michael Jordan, hang on to impossibly slippery objects like the comic book Spiderman, float through the sky like Superman, and move instantly from one place to another like my favorite, the Flash. But even more important, in dreams we can reconfigure reality around us. We usually don't realize how powerful this is because for most of us our dreams control us. We are whipsawed from place to place, time to time, in our dreams and sometimes wake up panting from the mental exertion. But when you stop to think of it objectively, as fearful as some of us may be about what we encounter in dreams, in truth we are the superheroes in the world in which we dream.

Now, just think of how much more powerful we would be if we could do at least two things. First, think of what we could achieve if we didn't reject the dream state as only a dream. Try it as an experiment and just say "no" to rejection. Begin your own psychic transformation by allowing yourself to believe that what you experienced in a dream was as real and as palpable as what you experience in everyday life. You can fly, walk on water, communicate with the spirits of the dead, communicate psychically, travel out of your body, and travel in time. You can control your own future in dreams once you know how to do it, and you can bring back from dreams exactly what you need to know to navigate in this everyday waking world.

Next, allow yourself to daydream. What if you could find a way to shut off your analytical overlay ability without actually going to sleep? What if the same possibilities that exist in dreams could inhabit your waking life? You would be able to communicate with a world of psychic phenomena where there are no logical limitations on what you could do, where you could go, or what you could see. Perhaps this is the limitless world Ingo Swann taught his remote viewers about and the world which he cautioned his reviewers not to inhabit. For example, I was particularly taken by Paul Smith's description of having remote-viewed a particularly beautiful place during a session with Ingo. The location was so alluring that while Smith was walking down a Manhattan street, he allowed his mind to float back there and the physical presence of that place became so real, Smith found himself falling over right on the street. He had come to the edge of an actual out-of-body experience. Unfortunately Times Square is not the best place to have one of those.

How many people have had or almost had an experience similar to Smith's? I know I have. Again, the power of harnessing this ability is enormous. If you didn't have to go to sleep to get in touch with your own psychic or telepathic abilities you would discover an aspect of yourself so powerful it would force you to redefine what you are. At the same time as you were redefining yourself, you would come to recognize that there was another reality or many other realities. You would not only become a self-aware telepathic, you would become something of a transdimensional being capable of navigating from this plane to other planes just like the shamans and medicine men of ancient civilizations.

Now, if you were one of the early investigators of remote viewing looking at this possibility thirty-five years ago, would you walk into the halls of Congress touting this possibility and asking for millions of dollars to prove it? Of course not. You might as well ask that chairman of a House or Senate committee to acknowledge the presence of UFOs. If you wanted to get funding for remote viewing and similar programs, you would do exactly what Hal Puthoff and Ingo Swann did and find a way to explain it scientifically, just like an engineering solution, so as to keep it grounded in our everyday existence. You would reverse engineer it.

But deep down inside you might not be seduced by the language of science. Part of you might accept the magnitude of what you were advocating. And ultimately you might come to accept the larger reality that not only are you telepathic, but that telepathy itself presumes that there are other universes, other planes of reality not explained by our laws of physics and natures. How do you get there? You know that once you do get there, you will partake of the limitless power of real human experience. You will be able to see the future, return to the past, communicate with others on a psychic level. Become better at everything you do. So how do you start? You can begin by a process known to the ancients, which we call lucid dreaming.

CHAPTER

7

LUCID DREAMING
INTO THE COLLECTIVE
GREAT LINK

How I Learned to Listen

Most people think that to be a talk show host you have to be a great talker. I'm here to tell you that's a myth. Sure there are hosts that can keep an audience entertained for an hour, maybe two, but after that, the romance fades away. Want to know what makes a good talk show host? You have to be a great listener. Years ago, someone said to me that the best salesperson is a buyer. Makes sense, doesn't it? How can you sell something if you don't like it enough to buy it? Similarly, the best talk show host is a listener. Why? Because as a talk show host you have to be a member of your own audience or else it simply doesn't click. So I trained myself to listen. I listen to my intuition and I listen to my guest who's talking. I've practiced listening ever since I was a kid. The military is a great training ground for listening. And I had to learn to listen when I was in the Navy because I was an officer who was a small gear in a great big machine. If the gear doesn't mesh, the machine stops. So I learned to listen.

When I got into TV broadcasting as a news producer, I learned to listen. Doing the news is all about listening. You hear an editor call out something that's coming over the teletype or, nowadays, the Internet, and you better know what that editor's saying. You're setting up an interview for an on-air reporter and you have to know what the interviewer is going to say. Is there a story? You don't have all day to figure that out. So I learned to listen as an on-the-job training thing. That's why when people ask me what it takes to get into broadcasting, to do a radio show, I say, practice listening to other people. Open your ears and let the other person speak. You will be amazed at what you hear. Try it out yourself for a week. Try it on your kids. Try it on your spouse. Try it on your colleagues at work. It's amazing what you will learn just by listening. You will hear more about what the other person wants you to know, what that person is feeling, hoping, afraid of, than you could possibly imagine. Here's a story from my own experience.

One of the first times I was ever told to keep quiet and listen was at a meeting I once had in college with the dean of students. We were setting up some student function, I forget what it was, but it required that we have a meeting with the dean of students to get permission. The club president who dragged me along told me in no uncertain terms that the dean likes to speak and doesn't like to be spoken to, especially by students. So, he said, just keep quiet. We got into the meeting and the dean started talking. She looked at him and talked. Looked at me and talked. He spoke, and I said absolutely nothing. I might have smiled, I might have nodded as if I knew what was going on, but I said absolutely nothing. A clam. Weeks

after the meeting I saw my friend planning the event and
he said to me, "You know, George, the dean said you were
one of the brightest students she'd ever spoken with." Les-
son learned and learned forever.

I am listening to a listener phone call from east of the
Rockies.

"Does any of this have anything to do with the end of
time?" the caller asks.

"The end of days?" I ask her back.

"When you're retiring," she says.

She reminds me what I have told audiences for the past few
years. I have said it on the air and I will say it right here. In
2012, the end of time according to the Mayan calendar, I have
said I will retire. I want to be on the air in May 2012, when we
encounter the end of time because I intend to report it as it
happens. And after that, I will stay on the air until they take me
out in a box.

The problem is that we really don't know what the Mayans
meant by the end of time. Did they mean that at a certain
point in May 2012 everything we know will be destroyed? Or
did they mean that one time period would end and another
would begin? There has been a lot of speculation about this.
One theory is that the Mayans knew that when the alignment
of stars or planets or our galaxy was in a certain position, it
would mark the beginning of a new age and the end of the existing one. Maybe that's why the calendar simply stopped. Another theory posits that in 2012 our solar system will be in
alignment with the black hole at the center of our galaxy and

the alignment will create different energy vectors that will create fundamental changes on our planet. Still another theory suggests that the end of time means the end of individualism as we know it, the end of one aspect of humanity and the beginning of another. In this theory, human beings evolve to a new state in which they become part of a hive mind, journeying into the collective and staying there for as long as they want to. That would indeed mark the end of one stage of human evolution and signal the beginning of a new one. There are those who tell us that the psychic powers and telecommunication abilities of Indigo Children and Crystal Children already represent the promise of that evolution. Or it maybe that in 2012, we will understand that we have the ability to travel in time and that time folds over upon itself.

This higher stage of human evolution won't happen exactly on April 30, or May 11, 2012, of course. But maybe that will be when we realize it has happened. Maybe the realization that we are evolving into and are closing with each other to form a collective mind has been gradually happening over the past hundred or so years. Shafica, for example, demonstrated the abilities of her subjects to link to some form of a collective of all existence in order to perceive auras around people, sense when certain events were about to happen, and even experience the sensation of being outside one's own body. The United States Army trained officers to travel along a signal line telepathically to a place where they were able to isolate images from distant locations and distant times. And these were practical applications of a theory that Carl Jung articulated, which presupposed the existence of a superuniversal collective of shared psychological information.

If we as a species are evolving to a shared mind or a Borglike collective, it's pretty clear not only that we've been doing it for almost a hundred and fifty years, but that we've always had this capability and probably exercised it more in primitive and indigenous cultures than we have after the Age of Industrialization. Ingo Swann's theory of analytical overlay explains this. Logic and language, the need to categorize and analyze, pigeonholes experiences and rejects those events that do not conform to established categories. This is just the opposite of what remote viewers are supposed to do: report on what they perceive without any analysis. However, the Age of Science and Industry, which began probably in the early Renaissance after the lines of trade and communication opened to the Middle East, taught analysis of events and testing for predictability. The constraints of logic and law channeled human experience and behavior into discrete patterns. And the religious wars that dominated the Reformation and Counter-Reformation condemned any spirituality that did not have the imprimatur of religious authorities.

People who reported psychic experiences or any form of telepathic communication were branded as witches and warlocks. In the early New England colonies, even those women who were thought to have extrasensory experiences were accused of communing with the Devil, tortured into confessions, and burned at the stake. The King James Bible demanded that witchcraft be forbidden.

Yet in pre-Christian societies the abilities of certain individuals to communicate with a collective so as to report on future events was treasured. These oracles were problem solvers, who not only made simple predictions but taught their supplicants to solve their own problems. Remember how the blind prophet Tiresias counseled Oedipus to examine the problems of his society by reaching into his own memory to the day he met an older man at a crossroads, struggled with him, and eventually killed him? That counseling led Oedipus to discover that the woman he married after his fateful encounter with the old king Laius was his own mother. Laius was his father. And Oedipus, by murdering his father and marrying his mother, had actually been the instrument of fate, the working out of a celestial plot. It didn't take a Condoleezza Rice, a Henry Kissenger, or a multibillion dollar think tank to solve the problems of that government. It took the insight of a blind prophet.

Similarly even during the post-Renaissance period, playwrights such as William Shakespeare and Christopher Marlowe catered to the Elizabethan audience's belief in an otherworldly presence. Dreams foretold the future for Shakespearean characters; ghostly spirits—like the apparition of Hamlet's murdered father—appeared on the parapets of castles; and a soothsayer wisely warned Julius Caesar to beware the Ides of March. In fact, it was rare when throughout its history, literature was not rampant with stories of prophetic dreams, messages carried by ghosts or spirits, or the abilities of characters to sense their own futures.

It is paradoxical, therefore, that throughout the history of Western civilization, the more government and religious authorities officially doubted the otherworldly abilities of people and even persecuted those who claimed such abilities, literature and popular belief belied what the authorities spouted. As author Joel Martin has pointed out, some of the greatest paradoxes took place right in the presidential quarters as Franklin Pierce, Abraham Lincoln, Woodrow Wilson, Ronald and Nancy Reagan, and even first lady Hillary Clinton all dabbled in the occult, the paranormal, or the world of psychic phenomena to receive impressions of the future or messages from the departed.

With the exception of the Lincolns and the Pierces, who lived during the "Great Age of Spiritualism" in the nineteenth century, most modern presidents took great pains to hide their interest in the paranormal. In Wilson's administration, prophet Edgar Cayce was secreted in and out of the White House. Nancy Reagan took great pains to conceal her reliance on the advice given by astrologer Joan Quigley, and the Clintons were the subjects of a derisive media after newspapers revealed that Hillary was working with Jean Houston to guide her imaginary conversations with former first lady Eleanor Roosevelt. In America, we like to keep our consorting with alternative realities a secret from the newspapers lest the average American, who most likely already believes in extrasensory perception, think that his or her political leaders are consorting with the Devil.

Thus, in the United States military, within our intelligence services, in private remote-viewing training programs across the country, and even within our own presidential living quarters, an active participation in what would have been called black magic 350 years ago is alive and well. As paradoxical as this may seem, there really is no mystery here. As my many talk show guests have pointed out, among them Dr. Michio Kaku, a graduate faculty member at the City College of New York, theoretical physics recognizes that there are multiple universes in which multiple versions of ourselves may exist with only minor differentiations. Dr. Max Tegmark, another theoretical physicist at MIT, has written that not only can it be shown that parallel universes exist, but that they may exist literally centimeters away from one another.

What does a theory of multiple universes have to do with our government's dual personality regarding the paranormal? I believe, and the remote-viewing program itself has demonstrated, that parallel universes and the possibility of one universe influencing another is a further manifestation of the Jungian collective unconscious. Moreover, I have a sneaking suspicion that the ability to traverse the gaps among universes so as to maneuver in time as well as space has long been known and is almost an accepted fact within certain areas of our military and civilian intelligence circles. I also believe that the United States is the only country where successful experiments in this field have been carried out.

Coast to Coast guest Uri Geller has said repeatedly that the Soviets during the last quarter of the twentieth century had experimented with telekinesis and other forms of psychic communication. It has also been suggested that the Israelis had their own psychic intelligence gathering programs, not to mention the British and possibly the French. It would stand to reason that if our military had scored successes in these fields and police departments sometimes sought the help of remote viewers and psychics to find missing clues, that other countries' intelligence programs researched in the same area.

Because there has been so much work in the area of psychic-teleportation, remote viewing, and related phenomena on the part of government and military agencies and because of the amount of taxpayer money spent to research in these areas, isn't it likely that somebody found out there's something there, something tangible, quantifiable, and reproducible? Might that something be the ability to migrate one's consciousness from one universe to another or to jump from one apparent timeline to another? Remember, in the same way that Dr. Bernie Siegal argued for the curative power of placebos in pharmaceutical testing by saying that if one person is cured by a placebo then placebos are real, so it is that even if only one person has actually managed to make a jump from our timeline to another or from our universe to a parallel universe, that other timeline and that other universe actually exist. And we know from Paul Smith's recounting of his adventures in his book *Reading the Enemy's Mind* that at least one person has made just such a psychic migration.

Ingo Swann's experiences also suggest that he managed to traverse whatever junction exists among universes on many different occasions, even journeying to the moon where he was observed causing a disturbance in the psychic force. Thus, if only one or two people can accomplish the feat of transmultiverse travel, then transmultiverse travel is a reality. Even better, transmultiverse travel is something all of us can experience because, again, according to both Paul Smith and Ingo Swann, this ability is as trainable as teaching someone to play piano. After all, it was the main purpose of the coordinate remote-viewing program from its inception that it was not meant for only the few psychically gifted members of the population, but an intelligence operation into which anyone could be brought and trained. As General Stubblebine explained to the new members of the remote-viewing group, anyone of them could be trained to bend the spoons he held up which, he said, he'd bent into balls of twisted metal with the power of his own mind.

If all of these individuals, and the hundreds of officers who went through the Army's remote-viewing program, in some way managed to follow a psychic signal to a great collective, a link of all human experience where past, present, and future merge, does it mean they managed to cross the boundary into other realities?

Consider this: Ingo Swann journeyed to the moon; Paul Smith journeyed not only to Saturn's moon Titan but also into the immediate future right here on Earth; Wilder Penfield's patients didn't just report memories of events in their distant past, they traveled there and experienced them concurrent with their conversations on the operating table. I am trying to make the case that these events show that these people and possibly hundreds of millions of people across the thousands of years of human history exercised an innate power to navigate themselves to some sort of collective storehouse of human experience. Some of this experience is entirely personal while other parts of this storehouse pertain to the human race as a whole. But whatever data was retrieved from the storehouse, the feat of navigating into and through it seems to be a common power that all human beings have.

If we all possess this ability to journey into this nexus of shared or collective human experience, how is it exercised? Jung said we automatically wield this ability in dreams even though we don't realize it. We wake up, sometimes shaken, sometimes, depressed, and sometimes quite happy over what we've dreamed about. However, in our waking state, dreams simply come and go absent any control on our part. They can be, as Dickens's Ebeneezer Scrooge complained, only the results of "undigested beef" or an "underdone potato." Dreams may also sometimes be the subconscious reflection of physical events in real life. For example, have you ever dreamed that you couldn't breathe and that you were choking only to wake up and find out that in fact your nose was stuffed up and you were gasping for air? It's happened to me. Friends have told me countless stories of dreams about thinking they were losing an arm and waking up to find their arm twisted in a painful position. Of course people have also talked about dreams of flying, being able to breathe underwater, and even walking on water. This leads me to wonder about what would happen if you could combine some sort of external stimulation to control your dreaming but still experience the power of dreaming. What powers would that control give you?

These questions and many more are the subject of a discipline called "lucid dreaming," the art or science of being able to control your dreams, remember them with great clarity, and even predetermine the kinds of tasks you want to perform in your dreams. According to author and researcher Dr. Stephen LaBerge, in the fall 1993 edition of *NightLight,* who defines lucid dreaming as "dreaming while knowing you are dreaming," the "mastery" of one's dreams has been a discipline practiced by Tibetan Buddhists for centuries. Because dreams are empowering, allowing people to live through their dreams the types of life choices and even fantasies they do not enjoy in their waking life, lucid dreaming provides a mechanism to exercise those fantasies in ways that, according to LaBerge, enable lucid dreamers to "rehearse" their future choices.

Lucid dreaming is not especially difficult, but it takes practice. You have to develop a mechanism to tell yourself that you're dreaming when you're dreaming so that you can make conscious decisions within your dreams to take specific actions. For example, a friend of mine, who wanted to test out the possibilities of lucid dreaming tried for many months to figure out a way to tell himself that he was dreaming when he was dreaming. But many times his dreams were so internally logical that there was no point at which he could say, "Hey, this is a dream." That is, until one windy night when he was on his boat and dreamed that the boat was traveling along a country road near where he used to live in New Jersey. It was a familiar road that he'd driven thousands of times to get to work and school. This time, however, the boat itself was traveling along the road as the lonesome whistle of a freight train echoed in the background. The wind was making the boat rock back and forth, a rocking that translated itself into the rocking of a truck with weak shocks making it sway along the road.

In his dream, my friend raised his head out of the hatch and saw a road. It was a dream, of course, but he was nevertheless struck by the fact that his boat was traveling along a country road. The dream's internal logic took over and he assumed that the boat was a flatbed trailer. But then, still as part of the dream, he looked out over the roadway and saw a lake in the distance. This wasn't the country road he remembered. And why was his boat on it? Where was the trailer pulling the boat?

In a flash—the speed of thought is faster than the speed of light—my friend asked himself, "What if I'm dreaming?" Then, in a leap of faith he took a leap. He said to himself, standing on the top rung of the hatchway ladder, "If I'm dreaming then I can fly." And with that he pushed himself off the ladder into the cabin. He floated, just like a feather, gently to the cabin deck. And then, with the train whistle still moaning in his dream—in New Jersey, where he and his wife used to live, there was a little-used freight train that rumbled through the town on an ancient track, its whistle piercing the early morning hours—my friend made his way down to the cabin to tell his wife that he was in a lucid dream state. What if, he actually thought to himself in his dream, he could make contact with his wife and the two of them could communicate in the dream? But the boat's cabin was no longer a cabin. It was the corridor of the passenger train they had once taken to cross the country after the 9-11 attacks. My friend, now aware that he was in a dream because he floated down under his own power, using his eyebrows to navigate, from the hatch top to the cabin deck, made his way down the corridor. He floated, swimming in the air, along the train corridor, looking for the Pullman berth where he would try to communicate with his wife. He was at the door to their berth. And that's when the dream ended and he was back in the main cabin of his boat where he had dozed off.

Having been there, he wanted to get back. Many people share the same kinds of feelings after vivid dreams in which they have achieved their life goals. On the one hand, it's a disappointment to wake up and realize that in the universe of your dream, you were at the top of the world. On the other hand, the fact that in your own mind is the capability to create that future, at least to me, overrides any disappointment. It's a different kind of spin on Bernie Siegal's argument that if a placebo manages to effect a cure of a patient with an incurable disease, that's no fluke—it means that the power of the mind is such that it cannot only overcome physical ailments, it can essentially re-create the future.

Such is the power of lucid dreaming, my *Coast to Coast* guest Dr. LaBerge says in his 1993 *NightLight* article, that dreamers can do what whatever they want. They are "free to do as they choose." But the reality of lucid dreaming goes beyond an illusion of choices because it extends into the perception of reality in which "the laws of physics and society are repealed." It is as if the dreamer has uncorked what LaBerge refers to as a "genie," who then serves the dreamer's every wish. Mere words cannot describe the potential of the exercise of this power because not only does it bestow on the dreamer superpowers, it also provides a conscious connection to the great link of all human knowledge where past, present, and future merge and where, I believe, human beings can traverse the corridors of the multiverse, switching timelines and futures like a train being rerouted out of the rail yard.

Lucid dreaming is but another way, I have been told by guests on my show, to train yourself in an awareness of your own consciousness. It's an acknowledgment that your mind is not bound by the physical realities of this world even though you feel the effects of gravity, make it a point not to walk in front of automobiles at an intersection, and obey traffic lights. It is a state of timelessness as well as physical limitlessness that, once skilled in the practice, we can enter almost at will just like the shamans or seers. If this was the state that the late Edgar Cayce entered to perceive distant events and the physical ailments of his clients that not even their doctors could detect, then, good news, you can, with some appropriate instruction, enter it as well and explore not only the possibilities of your own existence, but the entire multiverse. It's only a question of how.

CHAPTER

8

THE ART OF
LUCID DREAMING

H ow do you lucid dream, George?" my caller asks.
Dr. LaBerge can answer that question better
than I. Visit him on the Internet or replay the
Streamlink edition of *Coast* when he was a guest. But, I tell my
caller, here goes.

There are probably as many ways to learn lucid dreaming
as there are instructors ready to teach it. We've spent an entire
four-hour show on learning how to lucid dream without even
getting warmed up and still could not guarantee you the single
best way.

Learning how to lucid dream, I discovered, has more to do
with the way you live your life than any specific method of instruction. You will read that learning to lucid dream is learning
how to trick yourself to become aware that you're dreaming.
This is not as easy as it sounds, but there are ways to use your
habits in waking life to give yourself the cues you need to trigger that awareness during sleep.

Anyone teaching Dreaming 101 will explain that not only
do dreams have their own internal logical mechanism, dreaming itself may not be what you think it is. In dreams, even if
you are outside of yourself, literally watching yourself across a
room, your own dream logic tells you that this is okay, a perfectly acceptable reality. Unless you have a trigger that tells you
this can't be happening or make a statement that "I must be
dreaming," you accept the events in the dream as valid. But

that may only be half the issue. The other half is that the dream itself might be the out-of-body experience you sometimes think it is when you wake up. You travel back or forward in time, you encounter people who have passed away or younger versions of your self, or you bump into yourself in an entirely different future.

It's easy to argue that these are just unexpressed wishes that you don't daydream about during your waking hours. Psychotherapists also use these as a basis of communication between patient and the patient's subconscious, analyzing how the unexpressed wishes not only force their way into a patient's conscious mind but influence the way the person builds and maintains relationships. People who are frustrated about ambitions not being fulfilled or conflicted about what they really want to do versus what they have to do to earn a living can silently simmer, building up psychological pressures like the geothermic pressures underlying huge tectonic plates. Then, like the recent series of undersea quakes in the Indian Ocean, the psychological plates can shift along the fault lines, releasing tremendous destructive energy.

So it is with many people who go on day after day, shoving deeper into their psyches the real or imagined insults they receive daily until the pressure becomes too much. At its most extreme, when severely emotionally troubled individuals explode, we see headline-making cases such as workplace and school shootings.

Dreams might well be the release of the pressure valve for people in difficult emotional straits. We know, for example, that dreams serve a valuable psychological maintenance function by moving around short-term and long-term memories. Since we created computers in our own image, we can liken what takes place in dreams to the memory allocation programs for computer storage in which software maintenance programs re-allocate space on the drives for easier access to programs and certain types of data the user calls up on a daily basis. Long-term memories can get pushed into a section of our conscious-ness where they can reside without being disturbed by new information. Short-term memories, like a "most recent calls" button on a telephone, can stay as a reminder but then be for-gotten.

Psychiatrists will say that the allocation of memory and the movement of memories to new storage area is vital to a per-son's emotional well-being. And inasmuch as this memory storage allocation is either a function of or a correlative to dreaming, deprivation of one's dream state can lead to emo-tional impairment. Sometimes that impairment is so severe that serious neurotic symptoms can result. The emotional infra-structure of the person so impaired can even break down as a result of a lack of dreaming. Thus, it is no surprise that sleep deprivation is one of the interrogation techniques used by in-telligence agencies to break down resistant detainees.

I like to look at dreaming from another perspective, how-ever, the one Jung suggested in writings such as "The Phenom-enology of the Spirit in Fairy Tales," which is that the dream state is a gateway not just to the dreamer's own mind but to a larger collective unconscious. It is in this collective uncon-scious, a destination rather than a purely psychological mani-festation, that the dreamer encounters not just reflections from the dreamer's own mind, but actual forms or archetypes that are shared with humanity at large and refracted through the prism of individual cultural perceptions in much the same way that language itself acts as a prism of perception. In its most simple terms, there is a whole world out there waiting for the dreamer. Entering that world is a matter of dreaming. However, navigating through that world so as to make decisions consciously takes training and practice.

Understanding both the power and the importance of dreams, their necessity to the health of the individual's psyche, and their ability to empower individuals is a prerequisite for understanding the tremendous power lucid dreaming can provide. If you know how to lucid dream, you will ultimately know the enormous power that ancient seers and shamans wielded. And you wield this power in ways that will bring you an enormous understanding of how human beings think and react. It will, I dare say, make you a very potent individual. Lucid dreaming was the doorway my Aunt Shafica first realized existed when she began her studies of Edgar Cayce's work almost fifty years ago.

Lucid dreaming trainers have written that in order to begin the process, you have to condition yourself to link a certain conscious thought from your conscious state to your dream state. For example, let's say that you told yourself that every time you thought of your left hand, you would ask yourself if you were dreaming. If you did that enough times, one of those times might actually take place when you actually were dreaming. In that dream state, you might ask yourself if what you're doing or seeing is out of the ordinary. For example, you see yourself as a young child. You're the observer and not the child, but you know it is you. You think of your left hand and that reminds you to ask whether what you're seeing is out of the ordinary. It is. Therefore, your conscious mind concludes, this is likely a dream. At that point, as my friend did when he tried to fly, you might attempt to exercise one of your powers.

This is overly simplistic, I know, but it should give you an idea of the concept of trying to exercise your conscious will during the dream state. In fact, the practice of learning how to lucid dream is much more detailed.

Learning how to lucid dream is actually a form of psychological conditioning, training your mind to do something its protective mechanisms are programmed not to do. Because the memories we call up in dreams may be painful and because the raw and powerful emotions our social, more-governed lives force us to constrain are not so constrained in dreams, dreams can be dangerous if they control us rather than if we control them. In sleep, of course, to the nonlucid dreamer the dream controls. But, to protect ourselves psychologically from the power of the dream content—violence, raw sexual drives, absolute terror—our conscious mind not only erects barriers between the dream state and the waking state, but forgets the dreams so as not to upset whatever precarious balance allows us to navigate in a social world.

It is as if to say we are all Dr. Jekylls and Mr. Hydes. As Dr. Jekyll, we make our ways through life. But as Mr. Hyde we dream. Dr. Jekyll, however, wanting to get in touch with his evil twin that resided just below his consciousness, drank a potion that enabled the violent, vicious, and sociopathic Mr. Hyde to escape. Mr. Hyde caused havoc in the lives he touched, stalking through the streets by night in order to gratify his violent sexual pleasures. Ultimately, Mr. Hyde took over Dr. Jekyll in this moral tale of inner struggle between good and evil.

Although written as a fictional account, some neuroscientists and psychiatrists believe that this story is truer than fiction. There is a dark side to people. In many individuals, Dr.

Robert Keppel, the former Seattle detective who helped catch serial killer Ted Bundy and, years later, the Green River Killer, wrote in his book, *Signature Killers,* that there is a pathologically violent creature right beneath the surface of a person's mask of sanity. The overwhelming majority of people can control this dark side—Ted Bundy referred to it as "the entity"—but it is nevertheless present. To some extent, it informs the behavior of the individual in ways that might even be socially acceptable. The person can buy pornographic videos from the adult section of a video store. The individual can watch violent movies or play violent video games, sublimating his or her own urges into the actions of the characters on screen. Or the person can fantasize. As long as the behaviors don't break the surface tension of social norms, the person's fantasies are safe. But if an event occurs that unleashes the demon, the person's equilibrium may become upset and a new balance between the inner violent self and the socially acceptable self must be established. You would be surprised, Bob Keppel has said, how prevalent this is.

Part of these violent fantasies may manifest themselves in dreams where are there no social controls. Therefore, once a person begins the process of conditioning him- or herself to become self-aware in a dream state so as to tap the enormous power of the dream, the person also has to make sure not to open the door to his or her dark side, where reside the sometimes too natural violent fantasies that most people indulge in only in safe ways to release the tensions that build up in their daily lives. But in dreams monsters can reign and you can flee in terror from your worst projection only to wake up heaving for breath and awash in your own sweat. So be careful about unleashing a power that may be far bigger than you or that you have to come to understand in order to respect. But if you feel you know who you are and believe that lucid dreaming can help you gain more control over your life, then there are a number of procedures to help you do this.

Many lucid dream practitioners and trainers suggest that in order for you to exercise control of your dreams, you have to become a research scholar in your dreams first. You can do what Freud did. You can begin by writing down your dreams. Take a pen or pencil and a pad of paper or a notebook or even your trusty PDA and set them within easy reach of wherever you're sleeping. For most people it will be a night table, but it should be anywhere within a quick reach. For safety reasons, I strongly caution you against putting a pen or pencil under your pillow.

Pen and paper at the ready, train yourself that whenever you wake up from a dream you will jot down what you remember from that dream. Follow through on this. When you wake up, no matter how tired you are, write down whatever you remember about that dream. Don't stint on this. You don't have to be literate or even minimally articulate. Just get down on paper or into your PDA's memory your own memories of what took place in the dream. And be honest. This journal is only for your own eyes and should be completely private.

I myself wouldn't read my dream journal every single morning unless I had experienced a dream that was particularly unsettling. However, definitely review your dream journal every few days. Get into the habit of remembering certain recurring events in dreams. For example, a friend of mine has a recurring dream of always missing a certain class in school. This dream has recurred for so long and is so persistent, it has stayed with her through high school, college, and even into medical school. In fact, when she is under a lot of pressure she still has a dream that she encounters a patient she's completely forgotten about. She experiences a sense of panic, a familiar panic that awakens her panting and sweating from the dream. How much trouble is she in because she never went to that class? Why is she afraid to go to that class? And what will happen to the patient she has forgotten about?

Another friend of mine dreams about a dog he owns that always seems to escape or that he has neglected. He comes home to find the dog is gone, but it's a dog he only vaguely remembers having owned. It's a dog that, magically, he never walks though it never fouls up the apartment. It's a dog that reminds him of his own neglect. This person has owned dogs his entire life, but in the dream it's always the first dog he had as an adult. It's an unsettling dream that awakens him in a state of panic. Yet, although he no longer owns a dog in real life and although he knows in his conscious state that this is a recurring dream, the dream always traps him in its own logic while he tries to figure out, where is that dog?

If you discover in your journal that there is a recurring theme, maybe one whose recognition always eludes you in your waking state, that brings up a certain kind of emotion you feel when you wake up, write it down so as to associate the dream element with the emotion. Again, you're not supposed to be analytical. In fact, being analytical is the last step you want to take. You only want raw data, impressions, perceptions, and the emotions associated with them even if you list them.

Let the impressions themselves take you forward in your description of the dream. If you discover, as you write, that a particular real memory comes to mind, go with it and write it down. If the dream reminds you of something that's happening in your life at the present, write that down, too. The key point is to become aware of what you're dreaming as soon as you wake up and to write down whatever associations there are between your daily life and your dreams.

We dream many times a night and, more often than not, we usually either wake up and fall back to sleep, or move from dream state to nondream state through the night. In the course of a night, many dreams can be lost, their details only vaguely remembered, if at all, the next morning. This means that unless you give yourself a mechanism to wake up after each dream, the bulk of your dreams will either be forgotten or the vividness of the dream will be lost. So lucid dreaming researchers, such as Dr. Stephen LaBerge, suggest that you tell yourself as you're falling asleep each night that you will wake up after each dream. This is a process of autosuggestion, they explain, a programming of your own mind that your brain will wake up after each dream. It's like telling yourself that it's very important that you get up a certain hour. You set the alarm, but magically, you're already up before the alarm rings. Your autosuggestion has served as your alarm clock. This is the same process you have to go through to program yourself to wake up after each dream.

Once you've awakened and the dream is fresh in your mind, don't just lie there and allow yourself to fall back to sleep. That's what your body will want to do. After all, you need the sleep. But when you wake up after a dream, because your autosuggestion was effective, get right up and write down the dream. Don't let it fade away. Write down your most vivid impressions, noting all the unusual events that took place in the dream. Do this for a few weeks and you will begin to see the various signposts in your dreams that indicate you are dreaming. When you recognize them, don't forget to write down what each one made you feel. This is the association aspect of the dream that will allow you to recognize when you're dreaming even if you only have a surge of a certain type of emotion.

Finally, after you've written down your dream, you'll want to go back to sleep. When you do, try to focus on the different aspects of the dream you just had. Remember vividly the actual point in the dream that stands out, the signpost that you've just noted in your journal. Focus on this signpost, make the image indelible in your mind as you drift off. Hold it firm as you feel sleep take over. If you can do this repeatedly, you might be able to navigate yourself back into a similar dream state, in which, if you have been successful, you will recognize that you're in a dream.

Over the course of a few weeks or even a month, you'll probably begin to notice certain patterns. You may notice that certain people seem to call up certain types of dreams. You may see that certain types of dreams constantly recur and you have the same or similar responses to those dreams when you wake up. Discovering these types of patterns, themes, or recurring dream stories is exactly what you want to do. At some point, when you encounter that dog you haven't walked, the class you've never attended, or the client you don't deal with, you may, within the dream, turn around and say to yourself, "Hey, what if this is a dream." At that very moment, you are lucid dreaming.

Learning to lucid dream is a process wherein you document your life habits as well as your dreams. You focus on your habits because many times dreams can be deceiving in that they are built on certain life habits with only a few clues that the habits are plugged into situations that are illogical. These clues are the tip-offs that you're in a dream state. Knowing this, you can begin to compile a list of your life habits while you are compiling your dream journal.

Here's how to do it. Figure out your daily routines. For most of us, we get up at certain time, go through the same morning ritual each day, eat breakfast, and commute to work or to school. We get the kids off to school. We spend however many hours we need to at work, and then slog home, eat, we may or may not watch TV or study, and, by a certain hour, drop off to bed. We take the same routes to and from work or school or shopping, drive our cars in the same way each day, and engage in the same likes that enhance our lives. In short, our lives are built around routines.

Now if we take as a given that we dream what we live, we have a workbench test we can perform. What would happen if we took the routines that are our lives and added things to them so as to change the routines in a meaningful way? I'm not saying quit work or take your Harley on a road trip across Canada. However, I am saying that you should do something that you can use as a mnemonic device. In other words, if you add something to your routine, ask yourself when you recognize that you add it, "Am I dreaming?" This may sound strange, but think about it for a second. Let's say you move your wristwatch from one hand to the other. So if you look at your left wrist while getting onto the freeway, just as you do every day, and realize that your watch is on your right hand, you should ask yourself at that moment, "Am I dreaming?" If you're not, keep on going. However, you're training your conscious mind to ask the key question you're going to ask yourself in dreams.

Here's another trick. Place a Post-it note on which you've written "Am I dreaming?" on your mirror. At first it might annoy your spouse, or others who you live with, but ultimately everyone would get used to it. The point is not to bother your spouse but to get yourself into the process of asking whether you're dreaming. Imagine you are dreaming and you've trained yourself to look at the Post-it note and ask whether you're dreaming. You dream that you're standing by a mirror and, whoops, no Post-it note. Or you dream you are by the mirror and there is a Post-it note. You ask, "Am I dreaming?" and suddenly the answer is yes. You've done it. You're now at the beginning of a lucid dreaming episode.

You can also start wearing your watch to bed or putting a clock next to your pillow and staring at it while you fall asleep. Try to think of that clock to the exclusion of anything else as you drop off. This will take some doing, but try anyway. When you're nice and tired, at the onset of sleep, you're in what is sometimes called a hypnogogic state, where you actually hallucinate as your body muscles tense up in a mild paralysis. Your mind begins to wander and, if you don't recognize what's happening, your subconscious illogical mind floods your conscious mind with images. This is the transition from a hypnogogic state to a light sleep state. You actually may transition directly into a dream. If you've ever driven late at night when you're tired, you've probably had to fight off this state a number of times, trying to stay awake until the next coffee stop.

If you've trained yourself to look at a clock at your bedside as you begin to drift off, that image of the clock might just linger in your early dream state. Should that happen, try to make out the numbers on the clock. If the numbers seem strange or you can't make them out, that's one sign that you're dreaming. Numbers on a watch or clock simply cannot be recognized in a dream state. Therefore, if you're looking at the clock, which you've trained yourself to do, and can't make out any numbers, ask yourself, "Am I dreaming?" If you believe you are because you can't read what you're looking at, then you've achieved a lucid dream state and, in the world you're now in, you are the ruler.

Lucid dream researchers such as Dr. LaBerge and Lynn Levitan also suggest that from your dream journal, you try to identify what are known as "dreamsigns" or particular indicators from your dreams that tell you you are dreaming. A very good quick study guide where you can find a short course in lucid dream training, particularly in dreamsign identification is Erin Wamsley's "A Guide to Lucid Dreaming" on the Internet, where you will find Stephen LaBerge's dreamsign categories. LaBerge describes these categories as an Action, where either you or another character in your dream does something that is impossible in waking life, such as flying or floating, or even breathing underwater; a Context, where you find yourself in a place so strange, unfamiliar, or unknown it is not one you would associate with your waking life; Form, in which you or another character change shape or form, like growing or losing hair or taking on animal shapes; Awareness, in which you or a character you have some relationship with in the dream has an out-of-the-ordinary thought or power such as knowing something without being told it or having a memory about something that either never happened or is completely misplaced in time.

LaBerge suggests that in your dream journal you total up the number of dreamsigns and then divide by category and add up the number of times you recognized this category. This training is designed to trigger your awareness not just of signs but of the kinds of signs you encounter in your dreams. At some magic moment in a dream, you will recognize a dream-sign, an indicator that you are in a dream and, ideally, that recognition will be the beginning of a lucid dream.

The lucid dreaming experts tell us that a key step in experimenting with your dream is to move from the recognition stage—"Hey, I'm dreaming"—to engaging in the dream itself. That is, once you've realized you're in a dream, the technique is to navigate within that dream, prolonging it, and exercising the new powers that you have attained as a result of being in the dream. The lucid dreaming researchers tell their trainees not to be worried about the dream. After all, it is only a dream. You're not going anywhere. You're not having an out-of-body experience such that, if you're not careful, you won't come back. Others might say that dreams are actually voyages to a different place and that they can mark the nodes or transit points between this universe and parallel universes in which there are different timelines. Dreams themselves may create new timelines, environments where we can exercise our powers.

The nature of the lucid dream experience is for you to explore, whether only a dream or an actual trip to a parallel universe. But to make that exploration fruitful, you will first have to practice maintaining the dream so that you don't pop out of it, as my friend did, once you recognize that it is a dream. You may have the sense that the dream is slipping away, that you can't control it. In those instances, researchers say, try to focus on a detail of the dream. Focus on a face, on your immediate surroundings, or on any detail that stands out. This often helps to keep you in the dream.

The big question most people ask is, "Okay, now that I'm

dreaming, what do I do?" The answer is as simplistic as it is real. "Anything you want." After all, this is your dream. You're the one in control. My friend wanted to connect with his wife in his dream to see if they could communicate with each other in a dream state. Others try to reach loved ones as well. And this is something you can try. If you have a relationship with someone, try to visit them in the dream. You don't have to play by any rules. You don't have to be afraid of waking them up in the middle of the night. Communication with a friend or loved one, establishing a dream relationship, is one way to exercise the great powers that you have accrued during your lucid dream.

In your dream, you have the power to change the plot or the story. You are like a movie director. When you want to change to another scene or make a jump because you feel that this dream is fading, simply close your eyes. Pretend that you are going to sleep within the dream, researchers say, so that you effectively lucid dream within a lucid dream. When you next open your eyes within your dream, you will still be dreaming, but the scene and plot of the dream will change.

I have had this experience myself on at least one occasion that I can remember. What made it so weird and, on reflection, one tick shy of an actual lucid dream was that I remember musing, within the dream itself, about how the same segue to a story line kept taking place while I was lying in my own bed. You see, I dreamed I was lying in my own bed, and then I was in another place interacting with different sets of people. When the interactions became too intense, I was back in my own bed again as if nothing had happened, but with time reset just like what happened to Bill Murray in the movie *Groundhog Day*. In fact, that's how I wrote off the entire experience by thinking I was having a *Groundhog Day* dream. But I wasn't. I realize now that my vision of lying in bed each time the plot of the dream shifted was either a dream within a dream, which is to say that I was actually dreaming of lying in bed and that's what made me aware of the dream or I was waking up in a state where I was half asleep and immediately drifted back into a dream state to resume the dream. Either way, I now believe that I was very close to a lucid dream state without realizing it.

You can try to sustain your dream for as long as you are able, using any of the techniques the lucid dream researchers recommend. All researchers also recommend exploring your dream fully. Because you're in a world you've essentially created, even if that world happens to be an alternate universe that you've created out of the bits and pieces of the nexus of all human events or memories, you can almost define the realities of that world. For example, if you're beset by monsters or demons in that dream world, try confronting them. If you're lucid dreaming at that moment, you control. So ask yourself in your logical state what would happen if you summoned up the strength to tell off your boss or your spouse or the next-door neighbor from hell. Would that moment of empowerment transfer into your waking life by providing you the release of anxiety you need. I remember back in the 1950s that the television comedian Danny Thomas always had this skit on his variety show where he would be told off by someone. Then, he would walk away alone and in a monologue repeat what he would have said to the person who told him off had he summoned up the gumption to do so. It was a funny skit, usually ending up with the line, "Sure, that's what I should have said." You can do the same thing in your dream.

You can travel in time. You can look for someone from

your past or your future. You can imagine talking to your children as grown-ups or seeing yourself at some moment in your past. Relive an event. Change careers. Be the Walter Mitty in your own life. But at all times, be wary of engaging the dark side because, if shamanistic thinking is correct, as Carlos Castaneda described in his books on Don Juan, then you are not alone. Your allies and your enemies from the spirit world are out there and if you can see them in your dream vision, they most certainly can see you. So tread courageously but not in a foolhardy way. And remember at all times the phrase that the Knights of the Garter at the court of Edward III wore as a sash around their armor: "Honi soit qui mal y pense," or "Evil will come to him who thinks evil."

You should also visit the lucid dreaming website at members.aol.com/Aarenka/vision.html for Erin J. Wamsley's short course on lucid dreaming and draw on the resources Wamsley provides.

I have personally experienced the dark side. Some remote viewers from the military program also had glimpses of the dark side. They had intimations that what they were doing insofar as weaponizing an experience that should have brought them to a celebration of the great link rather than a narrow exploitation of it was morally wrong. I have read meaningful lines of poetry warning the complacent that when the soul's guardian sleeps, evil creeps in. And I have heard stories of how persons willingly can put themselves into a state where they are receptive to evil and, as a result, are possessed by it. That in itself warrants an exploration of the dangers inherent in opening up your spirit to the ravages of those who would turn it to the dark side.

CHAPTER

9

DOOM, THE COED, THE TEACHING ASSISTANT, AND THE DARK SIDE

A caller suggests, "But you can get yourself into a lot of trouble if you muck around with changing time."

And the caller is right, especially if you try to turn forces of good toward the dark side. In fact, as I found out the hard way, just poking around on the dark side can boomerang in ways you would never expect.

My friend and guest on *Coast to Coast*, national best-selling author, paranormal researcher, and radio host, Joel Martin, tells an incredible story of the Amityville Horror, a case he investigated at the time the story of the haunted house on Long Island was first in the news. He says that at first go-round, there was no ghost. The complete story was a hoax. It was fabricated as a story to enhance the value of a house, to exploit the story of the mass murder of the De Feo family perpetrated by the eldest son, Butch. After the story was first publicized by the new owners of the house, the Lutz family, who had moved in after the house was put back on the market, moved right out. They said the place was haunted by evil spirits, perhaps the spirits that had driven Butch Defeo to kill his parents and younger siblings. And author Jay Anson was writing a book to prove it.

Joel Martin had hosted Long Island parapsychologist Stephen Kaplan on his popular radio show, *Spectrum,* a number of times where Kaplan revealed that it was George Lutz who had called him, asking him to investigate the strange occult happenings at the residence. Kaplan explained to Joel, who subsequently became part of the investigation, that George Lutz's story seemed to change and evolve, which told him that he might have been researching the occult even before he bought the house. By the end of the first part of this tale, Joel Martin revealed to me in our on-air interview, even George Lutz pulled back from some of his claims about a haunted house.

In fact, as Joel Martin later revealed in his interview with me on *Coast to Coast,* the true story of the hoax finally came out with statements from Butch's defense attorney, William Weber, that he had actually created the story with George Lutz. The whole story had been made up. Joel says that Lutz bought a house that was simply too expensive and he had to get out from under the financial burden. So he and William Weber sat down and jointly came up with a story of a haunting and possession by demons. This was a story for profit, of course, delivered to Jay Anson for the book and subsequently for the feature film. But it was also a story to provide an evidentiary mechanism to get Butch Defeo back into court for a new trial, a version of "The Devil made me do it." But here is where story gets very strange.

The story of a house haunted by demons that terrorized a family was so compelling that even though the local police force called it a hoax, as did the local diocese, exorcists seemed to appear from out of the woodwork. One of them, Joel told me, was the very celebrated Father Malachi Martin. It was at the point that the exorcisms began that bad things began to happen. Joel Martin explains that it was as if Father Martin and the other paranormal practitioners opened up the heavy door of a pit into the other world, out of which flew all kinds of evil. Joel said that as an investigator, he experienced all sorts of malevolent events, including the death of his former wife as the result of a freak set of occurrences. The Amityville Horror story may have started out as a hoax, Joel explains, but the very act of opening a doorway into the world of dark spirits, the world of evil, let these spirits into our world where they began wreaking havoc in the lives of those circulating around the story. Amityville is a case in point. When you let your guard down, when you open a door—as I did with that Ouija board—you don't know who will come through it.

I heard another story about Malachi Martin, which was very instructive about the nature of evil and how it enters the world through the frivolous behavior of unwary individuals. This story was told to a friend of mine by one of his editors at a publishing company that specialized in textbooks on psychology. It seems that some years ago, at a very staid academic conference of psychologists and philosophers on the nature of evil, most of the afternoon attendees were nodding off their wine after the lunch banquet. I heard that even the most polite of the professors and scholars were having a hard time keeping awake, and an occasional snore could be heard from the speaker's podium as presenters tried to liven up their papers with jokes inserted at the last minute.

It was late in the day when Father Malachi Martin's group took the podium and gave their presentation on the nature of evil. They had video, they had slides, as I understood it. As one participant observed, by the time the group had delivered its paper, the audience, to the last academic, was sitting bolt upright, rigidly seized by a fear of what they had seen. If they had come to discuss the intellectual nature of evil, they were ill-prepared to stare into the very face of real evil and the way evil can overtake the unwary. Just what did they see?

If there is a doorway into Hell, a tiny corridor between dimensions through which demons can creep to prey on the souls of the living, Malachi Martin's presentation showed exactly where it was: in the psyches and souls of every individual. Each of us is capable of opening that door and without any warning, allowing the demons who reside on the other side to enter our psyches and make us their prey. What did Malichi Martin show his audience? He showed them actual photos of a young psychotherapist wanting to understand the nature of evil so she could help her patients, who, in a Faustian moment of hubris, stared at a swinging pendulum until she fell into a trance. Once there, she consciously focused on evil. Be careful what you ask for. She got much, much more than she bargained for. In fact, she so opened her psyche to evil, that evil entered her very being. For the ensuing few years, until she sought the help of Father Martin, she was possessed by an evil presence. It destroyed her will by preying on her like a virus until she could no longer function. She suffered physically, laboring from day to day under a crippling clinical depression that almost robbed her of her will to live. Her career suffered. She struggled emotionally with a pervasive sense of worthlessness. She was like a ship adrift. It would take months of therapy and exorcisms to rid this young woman of the demon that possessed her. Such was the power of evil once she opened herself up to it.

Needless to say, the academic audience watching videos of this woman, who had almost been transformed into a bizarre-looking creature, hearing the sounds of the demons inside her wailing their challenge to Father Martin, and seeing the palpable presence of evil within their very midst, recoiled in terror. They had come to study evil under a microscope, handle it with tweezers, discuss it as an abstract reality. But, in that very conference room, they stared evil in the face and had no words to describe it.

Suddenly evil was not an abstract concept but a living entity. Philosophy was fine, but this was like the chair you trip over in the dark rather than the erudite theoretical writings a graduate student would deconstruct for her doctoral thesis. Psychology was fine, too, but here was a subject who seemed to have gone beyond a traditional DSM description and into another realm. Her soul was suffering as well as her psyche. And, as the conference attendees saw, she had physical manifestations of a constellation of symptoms that bespoke of an invasion of her body from another realm. You can talk about evil, but when evil talks about you that's another story.

The real fear, of course, was not just that evil exists, but that it could enter this dimension via a gateway that seemed to be controllable by someone's volition. This patient had opened a door into darkness. She had thrown open a lock that, when closed, keeps evil out. When opened, even without the magical incantations of a witches' coven stirring a bubbling cauldron over a burning fire, the doorway let something menacingly real slip between dimensions and into our world. This presupposed the existence of another universe, an alternate reality, in which bad things existed who, given the opportunity, would prey on unsuspecting or willing inhabitants of our universe.

This person's experience presupposed something that Don Juan, the Yaqui Indian shaman, told author Carlos Castaneda, that in the other dimension that parallels ours, there are allies and enemies, allies on whom we can rely to protect us and enemies who shadow us in our daily lives and reach out to hurt us. Most of us, unaware of these allies or enemies, go about our daily lives manipulated by the moral gravitational pulls of warring entities. According to Don Juan, however, the war they fight is over individual human beings. We are the spoils of war as well as the prey. As dangerous as this sounds for those who go through life unaware of this war, life is even more precarious for those who become aware of the other dimension because they can see the dangers that lie underfoot. And, just like Bilbo and Frodo, who wore the one ring that ruled them all, once you see the enemies on the other side, you become a threat to them and they coalesce around you.

Don Juan's admonitions make sense. And it's reminiscent of what Ingo Swann told Axelrod, that once he was perceived by the alien entity on the moon's surface, he felt the alien knew who he was and where he could be found. Once you show yourself interdimensionally to an entity, whether it's via remote viewing an extraterrestrial or via some kind of Jungian trip to an alternate universe, you become identified and are vulnerable. Yet another way, equally precarious if not done with a heightened sense of security, is to lull whatever it is that guards you from evil into a false sense of security. This is also what Father Martin's patient did when she hypnotized herself with a swinging pendulum into accepting a vision of evil so as to study it more effectively.

This reminds me of another story my Navy pal told me about his college mate, Doom. Doom, as you can imagine, was a spooky cuss and had a very difficult time making himself attractive to girls: His haunted looks, bowl-shaped haircut that made him look like an old paintbrush, and very deep-set dark-ringed eyes often sent girls running in the opposite direction.

His gloomy personality didn't help, especially with the bouncy, perky cheerleader types he would plop himself next to in the student lounge. Doom, therefore, often said that he had to revert to forms of subterfuge in order to get girls to drop into his lap. One such method, aimed directly at a young woman's ego, was his very practiced skill at palm reading and fortune-telling.

As my friend described it, Doom would spy a likely candidate for a possible relationship, a candidate who would normally not only refuse to give him the time of day but would likely run screaming if he approached her after sundown, as if the devil were chasing her down the street. But Doom was used to this. He had cooties. People ran from him as a rule. But when Doom thought he had found the girl of his dreams, he would beg one of his acquaintances to either introduce him or drop the name of an acquaintance to get a conversation going. If he could convince this new object of his desires to take the first step by letting him take her hand, he would run it all the way to a meditative trance over a deck of tarot cards. At which point, until she awakened the following night with horrible dreams of having been fondled by desperate creature, Doom, quite literally, enjoyed his thirty-minute relationship. He was a very spooky character.

One day Doom crossed paths with a senior in one of his classes who awakened in him a passion he could not control. My friend said that Doom would go to his dorm room at night to pour out his soul about his obsession with this, according to my Navy friend, mind-blowing beauty with a sophistication and style not usually found among the undergraduates at this college. She wore not cutoffs and sweatshirts—the college uniform in early spring—but dresses cut just tight enough to drive a young man into a frenzy. She perched her sunglasses atop her head, just enough so they stayed put while promising at any moment to flop down on her nose, creating a tension of potential movement that bestowed on her a drama Doom would not have found while trolling among the cheerleaders, as he was wont to.

This woman, however, had her eye on big fish, the prelaw and premed types who, after she earned her MRS. degree, would provide her with the good life. She hung around not in the student lounge, but at the library, seemingly absorbed in study yet on display, as if through Bloomie's window, to the earnest preprofessionals studying *Gray's Anatomy,* and hers. Like Caliban in the pit or Grendel in his lair, Doom seethed in demonic rage. To her, he was as transparent as the invisible man, especially when she looked around as if hearing an echo when he managed to stutter out a "Hi, howayou" at the library's checkout desk where he had begun to lurk.

But Doom had a plan, he always did, which helped him bide the hopeless hours of frustration until the next psychology class when he could look on her from across the room as she stared at their hoary-headed professor, oblivious to Doom's malevolent ardor. He would wait for it, my friend said, wait for a tiny stream of light he knew would one day shine through the closed doorway of this woman's demeanor. Doom knew how to wait. And he knew where to wait. And the moment came, my friend told me, when the young suggestively dressed sophisticate, frantically digging through her shiny leather purse before a square-jawed trial-lawyer-to-be disappeared into the night, asked the wrinkly clad, question-mark-shaped awkward young man, whose form was just barely distinguishable at the very edge of her peripheral vision, "Do you have a pencil? I need one like really quick."

Like the spider who senses a juicy fly alight at the very edge of its web, Doom crept forward.

"Wait, let me look," he said.

And she paused as he slowly rifled through his looseleaf binder while the young woman stood on one foot and then the other until her prey, the pre-law hunk, was engulfed by darkness and she, more than likely, had made a mental note of his hours. She turned her attention back to Doom, a hint of recognition flashing across her face, and said, obviously before she thought about what she was doing, "You're in my psych class." The spider crept forward as the fly, unaware it was already stuck, planted its other feet on the web's surface.

By the time Doom had flattered her on the way she dressed, on her presence in the library, on her obvious maturity, and about his interest in exploring her fortune with her— just for curiosity's sake—she was intrigued. It was only part of the process thereafter as he got her to agree to walk him to his dorm to retrieve his tarot deck; process when he asked if she wanted to see real quick what the pictures meant; even quicker he took her hand to see if in her palm he could tell if she would interact with the cards, and finally a complete victory when she thought it was cool when he showed her how with two simple words he could make her fingertips stick together. In less than five minutes she was his. But it didn't end there.

Days later this young woman, strangely disheveled and no longer a sophisticated debutante, appeared in Doom's doorway, complaining that she was having strange dreams. They had begun after she had left Doom's room where he had laid out the tarot deck in a geometric pattern and foretold her immediate future. She had more than simply interacted with the cards, she had related to the images themselves, and had carried the interpretations of those images home with her that night. The images permeated her dreams at night and her thoughts in class. What, she asked, did Doom do to her?—because that night seemed like a bad dream. Doom, who had no concept of this young woman's susceptibility, only shrugged. "Didn't do nothing," he said, "'cep look at the cards."

My friend saw the young woman during the year a few times, now wearing sweats and a pony tail. No longer in smart-looking short dresses, no longer the perched sunglasses, and no longer the shiny pink toenails peeking through a pair of beaded sandals, she seemed to have sunk into one of the hundreds of mud ruts that ringed the suburban campus during the early spring torrential rainy season. And my friend didn't see her again until the following semester.

When they returned to campus in the fall, the young woman was once again the very picture of style. But there was a deliberateness to her, a focus, a maturity that seemed to affix itself to graduate students and faculty. Doom had since graduated and, my friend said, was on his way to another life. This young woman, however, had another chapter to her.

Rumor had it, my friend said, that she began showing up every afternoon in the office of one of her graduate teaching assistants (whom I'll call Mr. Wayne), who had taken a liking to her. She showed up every day, waltzing by the secretaries, who no longer tried to stop her, and sat herself down in the teaching assistant's chair until he came back from class. Then the door closed and folks could only imagine what must have been happening. Rumors traveled fast along the tiny campus, among the faculty as well as students, and soon the stories of the teaching assistant's dalliance with this young student reached the assistant's wife. Mr. Wayne was out the door inside of two months and looking for a place to live.

Soon, he, too, seemed to suffer a change for the worse. Now on his own, he at first lost his look of academic tweediness. His ties no longer matched his jacket. Then there was no jacket. Then there was no tie. His shirts starting exhibiting two-day wrinkles, then three-day wrinkles. He stopped shaving. The young sophisticate was soon gone, onto the new crop of MBA candidates like the chief of a hunting band of ancient North Americans cutting out the most tempting-looking specimen from a thundering herd of bison. The erstwhile tweedy teaching assistant was thus abandoned, like a derelict freighter adrift amid a floating colony of lichen in a sargasso sea.

My friend told me that Mr. Wayne soon began suffering from muscle stiffness and bouts of paralysis. It was strange, so the rumor circulated among the students, because Mr. Wayne was a young guy, a graduate student who could be trusted. Yet here he was, slowly making his way down the halls of the History Department with a cane for support. One cane one day cloned itself into two canes, each an auxiliary leg that Mr. Wayne leaned on for support. There was, my friend said, a haunted look of fear on the man's face as if he had been gripped by something terrible, whose essence he could not fathom. His muscles were losing strength, his legs were unable to support him, and it took greater and greater effort for him just to turn his head. It was progressive. Each day brought a more profound weakness until it was clear, even to Mr. Wayne in denial, that he was a sick man.

You would have thought that the legions of doctors who examined him would have come up with some diagnosis. But they couldn't. You would probably have said to this man that his symptoms where psychosomatic. He was displaying weakness to win back his wife, whose loyalty he had abused so badly by his romantic involvement with the young sophisticate. His wife did come back to him, at least for a while. She dressed him in the morning, trimmed the beard he had to grow because he could no longer shave himself, and even bathed him at night. Yet, whatever it was that held him in its grip would not let go.

In desperation Mr. Wayne sought the help of a member of the campus ministry whom I'll call Brother Pat. This New Ager tried to counsel him as well, but neither affirmations nor mantras had any effect. Finally the minister turned to an old friend who had become a legend in the downtown section of the city, Father Francis. It was wacky, the minister thought, so retro it almost was New Age in itself, but Father Francis, known among the inner-city residents for his exorcisms, was the only person the campus minister had not yet consulted. And you can only imagine Brother Pat's shock when the old priest said he wanted the minister to bring Mr. Wayne to the sacristy where he could talk to him quietly in the privacy of the cloakroom.

It didn't take Father Francis long to come up with his diagnosis, something neither the doctors at the fancy teaching hospital where Wayne underwent a battery of tests could figure out, nor any of the hip young psychotherapists who pored over their *DSMs* to find something they could bill him for, or, barring that, write up as a paper for the next regional conference. Father Francis said that Mr. Wayne was possessed. The campus minister was truly taken aback. "You mean he can turn his head all the way around?" he asked, more than half in jest. But Father Francis was adamant. If Mr. Wayne wanted help, there was only one way, and it wouldn't be pretty. Did Brother Pat want to help? Did he want to achieve a better understanding of the real nature of evil that had taken hold of Mr. Wayne? Was Brother Pat prepared to see the face of the true Enemy?

"Kewel," Brother Pat was reputed to have said.

But it was the wrong answer.

Father Francis admonished the campus minister that this wasn't an amusement park ride. Whatever Brother Pat would see would challenge him to the very core of his faith. It would so shock his belief system that he might not be able to emerge from this exorcism as his same old happy-go-lucky today-is-the-first-day-of-the-rest-of-your-life self. But the campus minister was gung-ho about taking on the bad guys, or as he called them, the morally challenged guys, and agreed to the process of self-reflection and spiritual purification Father Francis laid out for him. He admonished him further that any weak spot in the minister's resolve or blemish of guilt in his moral fiber over anything he had done in the past would be exploited by the demons he was about to confront. "Better," Father Francis had said, "not to allow curiosity to get the better of you and to stand away. In battle, and this is going to be a battle, you want the people you take with you to be strong so that you can worry about the enemy and not about your friends."

At first Brother Pat was tempted to dismiss Father Francis's warnings as over the top. After all, the campus minister had degrees in social work, counseling, and philosophy. He was a college administrator as well as an ordained minister and had worked with student health services for years. Mr. Wayne's case was a new wrinkle, however, and even if he did feel a moral twinge at Father Francis's warning, he had to see this for himself, albeit from a safe distance.

"Be warned," the old priest said, and, that same week, he began the exorcism ritual.

News of this, my friend said, had already leaked out all over campus. Whether it was the campus minister's office assistant, herself an undergraduate, who had blabbed it to a sorority sister, or one of the student interns who were always working at the ministry office, no one knew. Yet, by the end of that week, Mr. Wayne's exorcism was the topic of conversation in the student lounge, the cafeteria, and the coffee house. And the very popular Brother Pat's involvement was the campus buzz.

I'm not going to go into the gory details of the exorcism, how Brother Pat became involved with either the demon or his psychological perception of the demon; how the young woman became enamored of Brother Pat and whether it was the girl, the demon, or Brother Pat's belief in the demon that became the very face of evil that challenged his view of life; how Mr. Wayne, now completely paralyzed from the waist down, managed to throw off the effects of his possession; or, finally, how Brother Pat became so transformed by the process that he left campus to assist Father Francis in his exorcisms. All that is a story in itself.

Suffice it to say that when the dust cleared, the girl was gone, Mr. Wayne had gone back to live with an old aunt, who drove him to school every day, and the new head of the campus ministry was Rabbi Herschel, who spoke Latin and ancient Greek as well as Hebrew, played a mean electric guitar, and could accompany himself with klezmer tunes on his kazoo. Ya gotta love the seventies.

There is a moral to all of this that Father Malachi Martin explained to the assembled academics at the philosophy of evil conference. Father Martin said that evil wasn't just some academic theory or loose concept. Evil lives. Evil was as palpable as the chairs the conference attendees sat on. Evil invaded one's mind, one's body, and captured one's soul. The ancients knew this as did the medieval poet who described the image of a dragon guarding the treasure of the soul. When the soul's guardian sleeps, the poet wrote, evil enters. And so it was with the psychologist Father Martin treated. By putting herself to sleep and allowing evil to enter, she turned herself into a vessel for the very thing she was trying to understand so as to defeat it.

Malachi Martin and his colleagues provided chilling evidence that if there is a dimension of enemy spirits, demons, and pure evil, it's not just the stuff of myth or folktale but a real part of human consciousness. As such, maybe the process of remote viewing opens a door into that consciousness just enough that if handlers direct their psychic spies out of an evil intent, maybe it's the spies themselves who suffer.

Let's say that for some, if not most, of the early Army remote viewers, the experience itself, communicating with a world of infinite possibilities that stretched across time as well as space was, on a moral scale, more good than evil. In fact, let's say that the experience, because it put viewers in touch with the infinite, was per se good. One can only imagine what it must have been like for the more accomplished remote viewers as they realized that they were reaching beyond this time and space into a world of infinite possibilities. The more practiced of them, I'm sure, became almost methodological about this practice, now allowing themselves to deviate from the carrier signal so as to make sure there was no analytical overlay distorting what they perceived. But for others was there an emotional lift that they had to tamp down in order to accomplish their missions?

There are stories concerning specific remote viewers from the Army program, who ran into emotional difficulties. You have to wonder whether it was the awesome realization that human beings weren't bound by their own physical space or whether it was responsibility of limitless human potential that caused these problems. It has been theorized that the demands placed on psychic spies by the mission requirements of their assignments caused some of them to develop nervous disorders or made some of them too aware of the power at their disposal.

The commercialization of the remote viewing program into for-profit enterprises perhaps created additional problems. If Joel Martin is right, maybe there are gateways to the dark side that can be opened up just as easily by those exploring limitless power, the way Dr. Faustus did, who find that their own humanity distorts their ability to navigate in the multiverse. How can you protect venturers into this brave new world of multidimensional possibilities? Perhaps the realization of the unity of all creation is something that can help to keep psychic venturers away from the temptations of the dark side.

THE WRECK OF THE SS *EDMUND FITZGERALD*

We're all familiar with Gordon Lightfoot's classic ballad about the wreck of the Edmund Fitzgerald *on Lake Superior, also called Lake Gitchee Gumee. She disappeared from the* Arthur M. Anderson's *radar at 7:25* P.M., *on November 10, 1975, in what might have been a hundred mile an hour squall as she was making for the Detroit River with a cargo of Taconite pellets. The* Fitzgerald *was taking water and listing badly, had lost her radar, and had sustained damage to her deck. My sense, on the night of November 10, 1975, when I heard the news reports that the Coast Guard had been notified that a freighter had disappeared near Parisienne Island, was that we had a big news story. Perhaps the* Fitzgerald *had drifted too far inshore in the gale-force winds, too close to the shoals. Perhaps she was still afloat. Whatever the story might be, it could be a substantial one: survival at sea, lost at sea, the perfect storm.*

I was the television news producer that night at WJBK-TV in Detroit, the CBS local affiliate at that time, and when I heard the reports, I had an instinct, that's all it was, that it would be a major story in the making. In a newsroom, whether it be radio, TV, or print, you have to have your ears out for anything that smacks of a potential disaster because your audience wants to know about it. And the Coast Guard report that a vessel had disappeared from radar had all the elements of something potentially very important. It must have been an hour after the story was reported, maybe I even saw it come over the AP wire, but asked permission from the News Director, my boss, to get a news crew out to the shore of Lake Superior to cover this. My boss said no. My instincts rebelled. I knew, knew, *this was going to be a story and even though we had limited personnel that night, a stormy November night, I had to get on top of it. So I made what today would be called an "executive decision." I dispatched our news team—reporter Ron Sanders, cameraman Les Walden, and sound engineer Ken Sneer—to go to the lake shore to cover the story. My instincts were correct and we were the first team on the story and broke the news that the SS Edmund Fitzgerald foundered in a monster squall and went down with all twenty-nine hands. There were no survivors. Her last transmission at 7:10 P.M. to the SS Arthur M. Anderson, following ten miles behind her was, "We are holding our own." Ten minutes later she sank. This was one of the first major stories that I covered as a newsman and proved to me that my instincts were absolutely correct. I have gone with them ever since, sometimes in the face of logic itself.*

THE PRACTICE:
LEARNING HOW TO
REMOTE VIEW

ART BELL

My personal inspiration is the radio pioneer Art Bell. It was Art who transformed late-night radio into a discussion of the paranormal with callers from around the nation and around the world. It was Art Bell whose broadcasts with Whitley Strieber and Linda Moulton Howe brought the subjects of alien abduction, crop circles, and cattle mutilations to the attention of millions of radio listeners. Art still broadcasts out of his own studio in Pahrump, Nevada, and still talks about the night he and his late wife, the lovely Ramona, saw a huge flying triangle floating overhead. It made no noise, it didn't even seem to have any means of levitation, but hovered over Art and Ramona as if to acknowledge what he was talking about on the air was absolutely real. Then it floated away.

When I was the Nighthawk in St. Louis, I would listen to Art whenever I could. I was covering the paranormal with my guests, but Art was breaking new ground, telling America that there was another world out there, a world of ETs, ghosts, spirits, and communication from the dead. How I wished I could take over Coast to Coast *and reach the listening audience with my message of under-*

standing about the world of paranormal that Art was reaching. What I didn't know was that Art's health was giving him problems and that, after years on the radio, five, six, and sometimes seven nights a week, he was looking to take time off. So I began standing in for Art, broadcasting Coast to Coast *out of our studio in St. Louis. There were times when we didn't know if Art was going to be on or not and had to wait in the studio until the producers notified us that we had to step in. Finally, we began to firm up specific nights. And ultimately, I realized my dream of becoming the host of* Coast to Coast. *But you can still catch Art Bell himself on weekends.*

THE SETUP

My east of the Rockies line lights up and my producer cues me to take the call. It's John from Toledo. He's aggressive, wants to start having out-of-body experiences, but is afraid. "All this good versus evil theory is all very well," he says. "But how do you do this without putting yourself in danger?"

Good question, John.

You have to train yourself. You have to get psychically strong. If you're going to develop your psychic abilities all by your lonesome, you have to begin a regimen that will purify you and help to insulate you from the evil forces that will seek to penetrate your consciousness. Exercising your psychic abilities is an exercise in power. It flexes muscles that most people don't even know exist or try to deny their existence. Exercising your psychic power may also fly in the face of what organized religions tell us about the dangers of sorcery and witchcraft. Remote viewing, and the meditative purification processes that prepare one for it, are definitely not sorcery or witchcraft. In fact, forms of meditation, setting to rest for a period of time the logical cares of the day and troubles of the mind, are actually part of most forms of prayer. We don't call prayer meditation, necessarily, because prayer, at least in formal religions, is all about connecting with the Deity, as opposed to a kind of self-realization. In fact, if you want to be dogmatic about it, self-realization in Catholicism is a kind of primal sin, the realization that Lucifer came to, which set him in opposition to God.

But we don't want to go there right now.

For the present, traditional and organized hierarchical religion maintains that the act of praying is not purely a focused consciousness, not a form of meditation to heal thyself, but a connection to the Deity in such a way as to submit to the Divine Will. Through submission to that Will, there is an enhancement of the self because the penitent has surrendered him- or herself to the Divinity.

"Huh?" He says into the headpiece vibrating in my ear.

"Relax," I tell the caller. "We have a long night ahead. Just you and I on a rainy Christmas Eve here in L.A. talking about the power of good versus evil." I wish I were in the cave in St. Louis, though.

We don't have to compare meditation to prayer. For our purposes of ultimately traveling out of body, we just need to make sure of two big things. First, we want to be on the side of the light, not in the darkness. So we protect ourselves from the evil that can penetrate our souls when we're not looking. Second, if we do out-of-body, we want to make sure we have a body to come back to. That may sound funny, but if, as I believe there is, a world in which lost souls are floating around or a part of the multiverse where disembodied psyches must wait, you probably don't want to be consigned there. So how do you hold down the corporeal fort while you travel through time and space?

"A purification ritual?"

"You got it, caller."

If you are honest and pure and can connect with the ultimate purity of the universe, of all creation, your experience will be healthy and fulfilling. You may encounter, but will not be undone by, the creatures of darkness, your enemies, as Yaqui shaman Don Juan told author Carlos Castaneda.

Ultimately, to begin, you will need a partner, someone who will go to a distant location and set up something for you to find there. In some ways it will be like the taskers that Paul Smith described in *Reading the Enemy's Mind,* the coordinate keepers off whom the remote viewers pushed to find their targets. You will need to have your partner go to a remote location, where you will rendezvous with that person psychically at the appointed hour. But before you can even get there, you will need to prepare yourself mentally for joining what I call a "great link" of all consciousness. It's my version of Ingo Swann's matrix, the place where everything that ever was, is, and will be exists.

Joining the great link safely means surrounding yourself with a white protective light. To do that, you must begin with a spiritual exercise, psychic gymnastics, to bring your body, your mind, and your soul into harmony. The way athletes prepare themselves for competition—weight training, roadwork, positive attitude adjustment, endurance training—are all analogous to the way you have to prepare yourself. Actually, you are going into competition as well, psychic competition in which you will project your consciousness into the multiverse to pick up impressions from a place where all reality exists in a single state.

You are going to build up not only your endurance, because remote viewing and out-of-body adventures can be physically draining, but your psychological endurance and moral resiliency as well. You need to be on top of your game psychologically because you will experience events that will challenge what you have come to believe about the physical world. Think of the training that ancient medicine men must have gone through. They not only had to learn to be able to shed their everyday perception, but they had to be able to go into a form of a meditative state instantly to be able to communicate with the universe that Ingo Swann described. I am reminded of the trance state that Edgar Cayce entered when he wanted to remote view his subjects.

All of this took endurance, physical as well as spiritual. Shamans and seers had to learn not to allow the "Oh wow" nature of their experience to flood their perceptions and overwhelm their ability to perceive. They had to develop a spiritual resiliency so as to ward off the temptation to exploit the enormous power they tapped into for their own personal gain. And they had to learn humility in the face of the awesome reality that they encountered because of the power they wielded. Humility meant sublimating themselves to a greater whole, a spirit, or the Divinity.

What were the exercises and training regimens shamans and seers used to arm themselves for their psychic and spiritual journeys into the universe? Can you prepare yourself in similar ways?

I tell people who ask me that the very first process is kind of a purification ritual. You want to quiet your doubts and anxieties in preparation for your journey. And you want to practice getting yourself into a meditative state regularly so you can slip into it whenever you go to bed at night and to prepare yourself in the morning for the day's events. Here are the steps, which, I suggest, you should follow exactly in order for them to work.

A call on the Wild Card Line: "Is this a special technique you invented?"

"No," I tell the caller. "But just for simplicity's sake, let's call it the 'Noory Method' of getting yourself ready for the astral journeys that lie ahead."

STEP 1.
CHOOSE YOUR MANTRA: 2 WEEKS

You're going to carry this mantra with you for many years, possibly for the rest of your life. So choose carefully. This should be a phrase, or a word, very close to you with meaning that resonates through your whole being. Some people choose a prayer, others an affirmation, and still others only a name of a loved one. It doesn't have to be in English. It can be an "Our Father," an "Ave Maria," a phrase from the *I Ching*, or anything that suspends your daily concerns or frustrations.

I'm suggesting that you take two weeks to choose because it would be a good idea to try out your mantra before you settle on it. You need to remember it, of course, unlike the Woody Allen character who was calling his guru because he forgot his mantra. You need to do more than remember it, though. Your mantra has to become so much a part of your being that you will revert to it naturally in the morning on waking and at night as one of the last things you do before you go to sleep.

I can imagine what a caller would say at this point. She would probably say that I'm leaving everyone in the lurch here. I suggest two weeks to choose a mantra and hold out the possibility of a prayer or familiar phrase, but never tell you what to look for. Okay, fair enough, caller. Let's go to making your choice.

HOW TO CHOOSE YOUR MANTRA

Flip through your mental Rolodex. You're looking for words or phrases that inspire you. You're looking for associations with people or with parts of the rest of your life. Does "One day at a time" inspire you? How about "Easy does it"? Or just a simple "serenity?" We also talked about using messages from prayers or psalms. A friend of mine has as his mantra David's affirmation, "Yea though I walk through the Valley of the shadow of Death I will fear no evil," a powerful statement. Other people may simply affirm, "Thou art with me." While other people, for over a thousand years have simply repeated, "Hail, Mary, full of grace."

By repeating your mantra, it will, as you will see, connect ⋏ you with the great link of all existence. For this reason, and to provide you with the ultimate in spiritual armor as you venture out into the multiverse, you need a good connection. That connection is your mantra. It is your karmic PIN that, like the PIN on your cell phone, plugs you right into the correct full-duplex connection. Your spirit will venture out and, because your mantra is guarding the passageway, evil will not flow back in. Hence the importance of choosing your own, your very own, mantra that resonates with your spirit.

Your mantra will stay with you for the rest of your life. I say this seriously, caller. I know well the line of prayer that resonates for me in the Hail Mary when the penitent asks Mary to, "be with us now and at the moment of our death." Imagine the power of that prayer, asking Mary to stand by until the very moment when our soul is freed, to guide us into the hereafter. In this way, your mantra should evoke a response in you that can stretch beyond time and space into the fabric of all creation.

Here's an appropriate question: With all the possibilities of choice out there, prayer, aphorisms, affirmations, and the like, what's the best way to choose? I mean, do you make a stack of index cards, shuffle them, and then see what rises to the top? Do you ask your roommate, cubicle mate, or soul mate to help you choose? Do you just do an eenie, meenie, miney, mo? The short, and possibly the most confusing answer is, you should let your intuition be your guide. We'll cover an intuition workout exercise later on, but the best exercise to begin the process right away is to take the two weeks to see if your intuition will lead you to a sequence of words that resonate within your being. This is also the first step of your upcoming intuition workout, letting your inner psychic gyroscope—and all of us have one—guide your decision.

You will confront yourself with lingering doubts as you run through possible mantras. It is natural to doubt every decision you make. You may gravitate toward one mantra, but your rational mind will pull you toward another. You may feel better about one mantra, but you may ask yourself the very self-serving question, "Will this mantra get me more bennies than the other mantra?" Is that a small-minded question to ask?

Sure. Should you hate yourself for it and give up the whole operation? No. You're a human being taking the first steps out into the multiverse. It's natural to carry a lot of earthly baggage with you. You eventually will have the ability to jettison all temporal and mundane concerns to allow you to fly across time and space and partake of the vision of all creation in a single gulp. But first you have to build up your strength with your mantra.

You will try out a number of mantras as you home in on your choice. Like a baseball batter swings a number of bats to loosen his muscles and test out the heft, you will probably do the same, discarding the phrases that don't resonate. But whatever you do, don't tell your possible mantras to family, spouse, or friends. The whole point is that this is your karmic PIN, not a phrase that's up for discussion. Consider this a secret between you and God. Choose wisely, but choose boldly.

STEP 2.
NOW THAT YOU HAVE YOUR MANTRA

"Okay, George, I have the mantra. What do I do next?"

"Caller west of the Rockies, with your mantra in place you now begin your karmic fitness program."

I explain. This isn't as hard as it seems, but it does require some heavy lifting. You have to lift your karma from something soft and about which you probably have some doubt, up to the ear of the Creator. You're essentially doing the same kind of exercise you would do in a workout at the gym, repeating sets for various muscles, and upping your ability to lift heavier weights. For your mantra, repeat it in sets of three many times during the day. Just like lifting a weight once doesn't do as much as repetitions, saying your mantra once and leaving it alone doesn't do as much as letting it work through your karmic system.

In different religious services, you will see that certain prayers are repeated over and over again so that they work their way into the penitent's consciousness. Only when the prayer has reached the penitent's core does it work its power. And prayer is a very powerful thing.

Similarly, saying your mantra in threes many times a day has the same effect. As your repetitions increase, the saying of your mantra will begin to transform you into a spiritual conduit. You are contacting the universe, contacting the Creator. And don't be afraid of making contact too often. The Creator X is happy to hear from you. You are a terrestrial calling home on a karmic cell phone.

HOW TO BREATHE

I know that you've been doing this your whole life, in some fashion, but do you really know how to breathe? How many people, smokers included, only walk around taking shallow breaths and not thinking about how much air they're bringing in? They are not thinking about how much used-up air they're expelling either. If you inhale shallow breaths and exhale shallow breaths, or even hold your breath because you're too otherwise occupied to breathe evenly, then the net result is a buildup of used air.

Think of it this way: air you inhale is good air and air you exhale is foul air. This is even true if you're walking along Ventura Boulevard or downtown Broadway. Obviously, the cleaner the environment the cleaner the air, but learning how to breathe in a healthy way works in the Great Smoky Mountains just as it does on the Santa Monica Promenade. The premise is still that inhaled air is healthy and exhaled air is foul and un-healthy.

Working on this principle, you should purge your system of what's unhealthy and bathe your system in what's healthy. Translated into breathing patterns, it means that you should inhale a lot and exhale a lot. Take in lots of healthy oxygenated air—as much as you can, and exhale deoxygenated air—as much as you can. It means taking deep breaths and expelling all the used air out of your lungs. Sounds simple, right? But 90 percent of us don't do it. We have to learn how to do it. For some Eastern religious practices, children are taught from an early age how to breathe correctly so that by the time they con- ✗ nect with the universe, there is no question that healthy breathing is moving them along.

You also know this yourself. Ever feel very tired, especially after you've overeaten? What do you do? You yawn. Your oxy-gen balance system forced you to undertake a mighty exchange of air. That's all a yawn is, by the way, an exchange of air. Think of it this way, your body reflexively understands when it needs to move air along, but only does it under some kind of stress. Same thing when you feel sick to your stomach or just basically queasy. You yawn to try to ease the quease. Motion sickness on a plane? You usually begin to yawn. Same with sea-sickness.

Once you recognize this, you should make yourself aware of your ordinary everyday breathing habits. Do you:

Take shallow breaths as a rule?
Hold your breath for a little bit rather than expelling the
air out right away?

Constrict or constrain your breathing when you squeeze
    into tight places, like behind the wheel of your car?
Stutter breathe. Start a breath, hold it; then breathe in
    more, holding it; then expel air the same way?

If you find yourself doing any of these, it's time for an exercise in Breathing 101. Once you gain control of your breathing, you can integrate it with your mantra to get a powerful meditative shot.

Here's the simple exercise, the point of which is to make you aware of your breathing so that you can transform it to give you more oxygen than you normally receive and prepare you to visualize the nature of the air that's filling your lungs. Begin by recognizing how you breathe—shallow or haltingly. Next, at specific times during the day, practice taking very deep breaths. Learn what it feels like to fill your lungs with air completely. Without trying to strain any muscles, gradually take in as much air as possible and then completely expel it. Can you feel the difference between deep breathing and shallow breathing?

Even in your first practice sessions, sitting in front of your computer or behind the wheel of your car, try to notice how much more comfortable it makes you feel to take in lots of air. All that oxygen is good for you. Also notice how you feel when you expel as much air as possible from your lungs. You don't need to exhale shallowly or hold onto used air. Relax, air's free and there's a whole lot of it. So let it go out of your body because your next breath will take in a whole bunch more.

Next, now that you're getting used to the feel of completely expanded lungs, nice chest-full of air, set aside a time during the day to do regular breathing visualization exercises.

Make appointments with yourself to observe your breathing exercise times. Since breathing is something we do naturally, it may seem so strange to do breathing exercises at specific times of the day that you might overlook it. In order to avoid this, do what many therapists advise their patients and make a specific appointment with yourself. Pencil it in. Say that at eight every morning, you will spend fifteen minutes doing nothing but deep breathing exercises. Set another appointment for just after lunch each day. Make another appointment for after dinner. These exercise times will help you keep alert and resist the temptation to go into late afternoon and late evening mental slumps. Your morning exercise will make you sharper for the early morning hours.

When you've spent a few weeks getting used to your breathing exercise appointments, try to expand them to other parts of the day. In fact, focus on your breathing to increase your air intake whenever you can. Breathe deeply when you're behind the wheel or riding a commuter train to work. Practice breathing when you find yourself watching TV or, better, when you're listening to *Coast*. Practice when you're in front of your computer or reading a newspaper or a book. In fact, practice as much as you can so that deep breathing becomes second nature and helps oxygenate you in all of your activities.

VISUALIZATIONS

As deep breathing becomes second nature, you should start visualizing exactly what the air that you're breathing looks like. Think of the air you're inhaling as pure white and shiny. It's as clean as fresh laundry. Picture the brightness of the air as you breathe in. Imagine that your lungs are filled with a pure white atmosphere with no pollutants in it. That's the air that's going into your bloodstream and being carried to all parts of your body. Imagine that air filling your brain with fresh oxygen, reviving tired cells and restoring your mental alertness.

Now expel the used air. Imagine that it looks like diesel exhaust, full of toxins. This is a cleansing process. The clean, bright, clear air fills up your lungs and in exchange, your blood cells dump back toxic air, full of carbons. That air contains all of the pollutants your body is getting rid of, all the toxins that have built up. The entire process restores you, cleanses you. The more air you take in, the greater the cleansing effect. The more air you're able to expel, the more toxins you're able to purge. This is your exercise.

COMBINE YOUR MANTRA AND YOUR BREATHING EXERCISES

As a next step, you should combine saying your mantra with your breathing exercises. Breathe in, fill your lungs to the max, breathe out, and say your mantra quietly to yourself. Add your mantra to the breathing exercises you are already doing. Do it in the morning, after lunch, and after dinner. Do it right before you fall asleep. Let the practice of saying your mantra in coordination with your breathing become natural so that you are cleansing your system while saying your mantra. This will help to put you in tune with the universe so as to begin the next process—meditation.

THE MEDITATIVE STATE

Although many remote viewer instructional programs do not include any formal training in meditation, I think it's pretty important. We're going to bring together everything we've done so far, the breathing, the visualization, and the mantra, so as to form a link, like an Internet connection, to the universe.

Begin by closing your eyes, getting into a comfortable sitting or reclining position, doing your deep breathing exercise, and repeating your mantra, keeping at it for twenty minutes. You'll find that opening the link will become much faster, eventually, but in the beginning, allow yourself twenty minutes. Say your mantra over and over again in sets of three, while deep breathing, for the full twenty minutes.

You will find, as you do this, that your mind will want to wander. The trick is not to let yourself hook onto a thought. You want to discard all thoughts. You only want to focus on your mantra because that mantra, and the associated breathing, is the mechanism that will connect you to the larger multiverse. Therefore, you have to discard the daily thoughts that will inevitably float in so as to intrude on your consciousness. You may think of what happened that day or what is about to happen later in the day. You may think about being hungry or an argument that you're having at work or at home. You may be thinking about a homework assignment or a major project at work. Or you may even start to fantasize about the person who works two cubicles over from you. Thoughts will inevitably find their way in and you have to find the means to send them on their way out. This is the hardest part of the process, but you can do it.

So begin by closing your eyes, starting the breathing cycle, and visualizing the clean air coming in and the toxic air flowing out. Imagine it is cleansing your entire body. And then, slowly, with every exhale, repeat your mantra under your breath. Let the rhythm of the mantra take you over and the cleansing breaths of air sustain you from inhalation to inhalation.

You are saying your mantra in threes, over and over again for twenty minutes. Errant thoughts may find their ways into your consciousness from the very beginning. How do you discard them? You can't tell yourself you won't think about anything because you most certainly will. The trick is not to build a barrier between yourself and reality. It is to develop a way to let errant thoughts float away.

Realize that essentially you have two minds. You have a mind with thoughts always chattering away inside, call it the "monkey mind," and a mind that can encompass the universe, "the big mind." When you're in your meditative mantra state, you want to let your big mind take over because that's the mind that communicates directly with the universe and the Creator. Your monkey mind will always try to intrude on the big mind. You have to find a way to slip the chattering out before it creates too much noise. Here's a way that I do it.

You are breathing in, filling your lungs with clean air. You are exhaling, sending toxins out of your system. An errant thought creeps in. Don't fight it. Let it come. But as you take that deep exhale, expelling all the toxic air, expel the thought with it. That's right. Thoughts come in, but you breathe them out along with the air. By concentrating on the thoughts going out instead of the thoughts themselves, you are ridding your mind of the everyday concerns that keep you trapped in the here and now.

Alternatively, you can close your eyes, begin your deep inhaling and exhaling and as thoughts flow in, picture them flowing out just like leaves on a slowly moving stream or river. Keep picturing the river and the leaves on it. Your thoughts are the leaves and they are floating away. Let them go no matter what emotions a single thought may evoke.

You will find as you do this thought discarding and repeating of your mantra that you will see a void, a space between thoughts. This is a kind of private nirvana, a connection to the great link. You will see it, experience it, embrace the silence that is the great link where all that exists is you through your mantra and the rest of the universe.

After twenty minutes a session, you should stop. Try for twenty minutes a day at first, but work up to getting millions of repetitions of your mantra into the Creator's ear. Believe that the Creator wants you to have your mantra, your connection with the Divine, to be the last sound resonating in your being as you fall asleep or in times of trouble. Use your mantra and your ability to discard everyday emotions at other times, too. Try it when you're stuck in traffic on a freeway interchange or at a light. Try it during the crush of a subway or commuter train rush hour. You are knocking on heaven's door and connecting with the other side. This is your ultimate long distance call, your vine out of trouble.

Say your mantra when you can't sleep and it's the middle of the night when the darkest of terrors seize you. You're behind on the job, you have people after your job, you have a boss that's looking to promote her friend over you, and you are up for an evaluation that you know you'll fail. No one understands the pressures you're under, least of all your family. There are forces out there who want to crush you. And it is at night when these fears creep up from the darkness and surround you, keeping you awake and confronting you with problems no human being can solve.

At this very time, you must begin your mantra, associating it with times of trouble. Your mantra, enabling you to make that connection with the great link, with your Creator, will be your strength. This is a tapping into power, it is a way for you to become more intuitive, more in touch with the real forces around you, and more able to draw on your own inner re-sources to help you overcome all of your own fears that are de-feating you.

Practice doing this as an exercise for at least twenty min-utes a session: breathing, repeating your mantra in threes, and letting all of your thoughts float away. Don't question this, don't let your doubts clutter your mind, and don't wait expec-tantly for magic to happen. When the magic happens, and it will, you won't even notice it consciously because you will have already moved on to a higher, more accepting, level of con-sciousness. You will, through your mantra and your psychic connection to the Creator, discard much of your everyday anger and frustration at life. You will simply have moved on. And this is the stage that prepares you for listening to an en-tirely other channel.

There is no point at which you will stop this exercise. Ulti-mately, this is your spiritual lifestyle, more than it is a diet. This will transform you, even if this is all you do of a night, a morning, or at times of stress. You will be better for this be-cause you will have made a connection to the vastness of the universe beyond. But, as I tell my listening audience and all of those on Christmas Eve dialing the phone to catch one of my open lines, wait, there's more. Much, much more.

BECOMING INTUITIVE

LISTENING TO CALLERS

When you learn to listen in this broadcasting business, you learn how to know when an earnest storyteller relates something to you that he or she believes is true. The story doesn't have to be true, but just from the way the person tells it, you know that inside that person's mind there is a kernel of truth. Just as easily, you can sense when someone is fabricating. I can't tell you what part is intuition talking to me or what part is simple experience from having listened to people most of my life. I only know that I can often tell right from the outset if someone believes the story she's telling or whether he is consciously framing a tale. Either way, my response is to be polite, listen, and find the elements in the story that will reveal that the person doesn't believe it or that the person truly does. Some of my favorite storytellers are the truckers who call me from the road with tales they've heard or experiences they've had. I sometimes will open a trucker hotline to hear what the drivers of the big semis have to say about life.

Here's one. Ever driven on the Pennsylvania Turnpike, one of the oldest turnpikes in the country and, in parts, one of the most treacherous? As you approach the Al-

leghenies, the PA Pike makes these long curves, which tighten as you get into a series of tunnels under the mountains themselves. Make this trip during a driving ice storm with a semi in the next narrow lane, its rear wheels throwing up ice onto your windshield, blinding you as the road turns sharply into a tunnel and your wheels slip on the ice-packed asphalt surface, and you'll know that you're between two worlds. This the kind of night my callers from the road have known for decades. It was just such a night when one of my trucker callers told me that he saw a figure draped in black just off to the edge of the road as he made the turn into a tunnel. The driver swears that the figure he saw was the Grim Reaper itself.

"So tell me more about your aunt, George," a caller on the Wild Card asks. "What did she say about intuition?"

There is a light rain falling over Los Angeles now. Outside the studio, in the early hours, traffic has dwindled to only an occasional passing car, its windshield wipers on delay as it penetrates the mist. The temperature has dropped, even though this is Southern California, and without the building heat, we'd be shivering inside the studio. On the East Coast, I know, children are making their first stirrings, dreaming about what they're going to wake up to.

"I mean," the caller continues, "did she say how to get intuition or only that you're born with it."

"Both," I tell my caller. "There are people who are naturally intuitive and who know that from the time they're very young. And there are those who have to be taught to listen to the intuition they already have."

This perplexes many people, but it's quite elementary. Think of it this way. Your intuition, and all of us have it, is your automatic connection to your Creator. New Age types say that intuition is that very small voice that invariably, when you look back on it, has told you the truth. Traditional religion says that the "still small voice" is the voice of God, the voice of the Creator, who whispers the truth to you every moment of your life. But how do you condition yourself to hear that voice? And once you hear it, how can you condition yourself to listen to the voice? This is a two-step process. Let's deal with the first.

Remember the analogy of the monkey mind and the big mind? Consider that the monkey mind, the chattering mind, is perfectly capable of making the intuitive connection to the larger universe, the great link. However, the only way the chattering mind can make that connection is like a dial-up connection to the Internet. It's slow, it's iffy, it's filled with static, and many times you get a disconnect message and have to start all over again. The line is always there for you to dial, but after a while, it's so tedious to keep dialing, you simply give up, grab something from the fridge, plunk down on the couch, zap the remote, and start flipping channels. Your brain goes numb.

How about if instead of trying to use dial-up, you could make a broadband connection to the great link? Your intuition, instead of a dial-up, is like DSL or cable. It's always on. You just have to figure out how to hear it. That's the entire point of learning how to condition your intuition to recognize the voice you're hearing. Once recognized, you have to train yourself to trust it.

I tell my callers that people get intuition feedback every

day of their lives and every minute of every day even when they are sleeping. Dreams, too, are facets of intuition, only we dismiss them because we've been told since childhood that dreams are only fabrications of our imagination. But our imagination is intuitive as well.

If we are getting intuition feedback during every moment of our existence, what do we do with it? Better, how can we capitalize on it and turn it into that sixth sense or fabled third eye? We can, but we have to set our sensory internal modem to recognize the intuition signal and then configure our psychological router to deliver that signal to the right places.

The first step is to recognize that our intuition is like a steady stream of data that we've been taught since childhood to disregard because it's essentially illogical. They burned witches, didn't they? Why? Because witches, we were told, listened to other voices that told them when to zig right or zag left. Those other voices, the moral inquisitors said, were the voices of the Devil. Therefore, if you don't do what people in authority tell you to do and listen to your inner self, you're a burnable witch and so had better turn off that inner voice. I'm here to tell you that the poor victims they burned probably weren't witches. And I'm here to say that deciding for yourself, rather than listening to authority automatically, is probably the best thing to do. Authority usually has authority's best interests at heart, not yours. Accordingly, you should listen to your inner self. I say this, paradoxically, as an authority.

That being said, how do you listen to your inner self? Usually, after years of conditioning the other way, it's tough to wake up one morning, declare that you've turned over a new leaf, and decide that from this day forward you'll only listen to your inner self. Try doing that in your cubicle at the office while Sally Supervisor and Mike Manager are glaring at you through the entryway and you'll see what I mean. Because of your years of conditioning, you probably have to recondition yourself to listen to your inner self.

Listening to yourself is a passive exercise. The act of listening is not something you need to turn on because it is always on. You have to learn to recognize the instinct signal that is always sending you information. It is faint, so we have to learn how to amplify it, and discriminate it from the rest of the data stream we process every day. You have to begin by believing that your intuition is already active and that all you have to do is let it reach you.

Perhaps the simplest way of putting it is "Don't try and don't deny." These are two sides of the same coin. The "don't try" side means you should not try to be intuitive. You already are. The more you try to make something happen, to force yourself to see something that may or may not be there, the more you are contorting your stream of information. You have to relax into it and let an inner voice guide you. It won't always be right and may even be more wrong than right in the beginning, but ultimately, through a combination of experience and perception, you will begin to recognize when your intuition is talking to you.

The other side of the coin is "don't deny." Sometimes people are afraid of their own intuition, especially when they feel they're picking up news that's either too good or too foreboding. So they deny. And guess what? If it's something good, they can miss the opportunity. If it's something dangerous that they could have avoided, they miss that chance as well.

I once read an article by a professor of management at the Harvard Business School in which he said that in business situations, people are afraid to be paranoid. But, he argued, paranoia was probably a most healthy emotional state because most people in cutthroat management situations have a particularly keen sense of intuition that's always warning them of the knife poised just between their shoulder blades. Deny your intuition about someone who's out for your job and who has no compunctions about tripping up your big project and you deny the huge green monster that's lurking just on the other side of the elevator door. Therefore, deny what your intuition is telling you at your own peril.

If we begin with the rule that forcing yourself to pick up something means you will often miss what's really there, and denying what you sense also means you are missing what's there, what's left? Simply this: Trust that if you look at the situations you confront every day without trying to color them or tell yourself you're seeing something when you're not, you will probably develop what you can call a Zen of unknowing. This is a kind of neutral, almost colorless view of what's around you. Negate the value judgments "good" and "bad," because they color the way you see things. Try to gray out your emotional discriminators so that the properties of who and what you see resolve themselves into their own colors. You will, over time, come to see that you will develop a sense about things, an ability to make predictions about things that come true more often than not. This ability to predict, to see something new in the situations that confront you every day is your intuition at work.

There are also exercises you can do to stretch your ability that go from very basic to highly involved. Here's one that simply gets you in touch with your environment, the people who populate your life, and your position in the space that is your life. It's called a "life space" exercise. You begin by closing your eyes, breathing deeply so as to completely flood yourself with oxygen, and repeating your mantra. You do this, practicing discarding all everyday thoughts as if they were leaves floating away on a stream. And then as you do this, you try to imagine your life as a physical space around you. What to you see? Who is in that space? Are you outside, inside, or in some undefined space? Don't force it. Stay in that space, however, until you can describe it to yourself. Then open your eyes and write down what you've seen. For many people, this is their first shot at remote viewing.

My highly inspirational radio guest Wayne Dyer has said that intuition is a very powerful force, which, if you know how to recognize it, can help you shape your own future in tremendous ways. He says that we are in far greater control of our lives than we dare admit. In fact, much of what he urges his listeners and readers to do is to admit that they have the power to shape their own lives. He teaches people to look at ways in which what they want or don't want actually shapes what happens to them. For example, an everyday exercise in this reality might be a simple parking space test.

We all look for the perfect parking space. Whether on a side street in Manhattan, Queens, or Brooklyn or just off of Melrose or Doheny Drive in Beverly Hills, when we're driving someplace, we want to be able to park. Ever pull into a crowded parking structure in a shopping center with a feeling of dread that you've paid your six bucks but will never be able to find a space? I have. Here's an exercise just for that situation. Wayne Dyer says you can create your future. So do it by telling yourself where you will find your parking space. Sound ridiculous? Not so. As you pull up to the structure, or along the side streets, try to let your parking space call out to you, draw you to it. Don't force it, but don't deny it. Your intuition will call you and you should go right to it. Sometimes this will work. Sometimes it won't. But the trick is not to give up on it. Ultimately, you will beat the law of averages so soundly that you will be able to amaze your friends and confound your enemies with your demonstration of intuition.

Here's another quickie that a couple of friends of mine do every year between Thanksgiving and New Year's Day. I call it the calendar exercise. You begin by searching out the calendars in a bookstore or catalog or wherever you like to shop for calendars. When you do this, try to open your mind. Don't just go for the same old every year, scan the racks for something that seems to call out to you. Is it the NFL calendar, a wooden boat calendar, a South Seas or a Hieronymus Bosch calendar? Is it your favorite expressions of Marilyn Monroe or classic scenes from Peanuts? Whatever it is, don't just pick one and shut down. Let your mind and hands wander over all types of calendars as if they're speaking to you. If you can, thumb through the months quickly, letting the calendar call out the future. Do this enough and the shape of different futures will become clear to you.

I've described a completely intuitive process that most people perform when they look for calendars, but without realizing it. Many people just say they like the pictures, like the photos of their favorite stars or cars, love the settings of the boats or the weather scenes or old barns in New England, like the fuzzy or friendly animals, or simply like the colors. In reality, people are exercising their intuitive sides. You can do this more actively by recognizing that you have feelings generated by seeing the pictures of the different months, have emotional reactions to them, and allowing these feelings to resonate. Pretty soon, you'll be able to sense things about the different futures from the calendars themselves and even, my friends say, exercise some control over the future by choosing one calendar over the other.

Sometimes, at the end of a year, you will know what things are coming up in an ensuing year. It's fun, and also great practice, to take what you believe you will encounter in a year and throw it against the calendar you're looking at. What does a certain month tell you about the prospects of a job interview or a promotion? What might the personality of your newborn baby, due in a September or October, be from what you can see in that month? Can you choose a calendar with a month that resonates positively or one that resonates negatively? Given that you don't control what pictures a calendar maker prints for a certain month, you might be able to choose a calendar with months that seem more positive than negative. In so doing, you can say to yourself that your intuition is guiding you to control your future.

There's nothing really magic about this process so far. If the theories of the remote viewing practitioners back in the day are correct, all you are doing is using the photo and the emotions you feel to bounce off the matrix of all reality in which the past, present, and future all coexist. You probably can't predict exactly what will happen to you on a certain day of the year, but you can say that because you have emotion A or B when you look at a certain picture, that's a future to seek or avoid. It's simply using and not denying that you have an intuitive sense about a certain image, a sense that guides you to believe something about the future indicated by that image. You're not worshiping symbols, only looking at them as guideposts for your own feelings.

Beyond the calendar test, there are other ways to let images focus what you are already thinking and feeling. Here's one I like. Does the real estate pull-out section of your local newspaper contain an "open house guide?" If so, you can use it to try out questions about your future and the alternate futures you might inhabit. You can fathom what your intuition tells you about certain photos, settings, or places and what might lie in store for you as a person, even if you're not actually buying or renting a house or apartment.

Begin, just as you begin every exercise, by chanting your mantra and letting your daily concerns and thoughts float away on the river. Now instead of just picturing your life as a space around you, try to imagine what it looks like, where you are, and how you relate to that space. Try to be more specific and picture yourself in a physical structure. Is it a house, a room in a house, an office, a building? What are the rooms like? What are the colors? Are you alone? Walk through the rooms, if a physical structure, and let your imagination stretch. Discard all negative thoughts and discard any voices that tell you this can't be happening. Inside your own imagination you are the monarch of all you want to survey. Ask yourself who you are in that house, office, or building. Repeat this exercise for a week or at least until the next weekend real estate guide comes out in the local paper.

After having done the life-space part of the exercise, flip through the real estate guide and look for the types of properties that most closely resemble the experience you had in your life space. See if any of them speak to you, call out to, or indicate to you in some way that perhaps a future is there. Maybe somewhere in the multiverse another incarnation or manifestation of you is inhabiting one of those houses or apartments. Or maybe you will have a future in one of those spaces. You don't have to identify what it is that made that structure pop into your imagination or what made you recognize it after the first part of this exercise. It is enough that your intuition told you there was something there.

The Open-House Test

In Los Angeles, this is where the fun starts. It was in Los Angeles that a couple of my friends played out this exercise in intuition, and found that it was almost frighteningly prophetic. Here is the basic question they asked: "What does the future hold in store?" Seems innocuous enough. We ask that every time we open a fortune cookie at a Chinese restaurant. But if we begin to refine that question, as my friends did, then it gets interesting. For example, what does the future hold in store for us in that house in the picture? What am I looking for from the future and where will I be able to find it? What does my intuition tell me about what I will find out today?

These are some of the questions they began asking. Then they played a game. They got specific about what they "intended" to find out from their open-house forays. And they parlayed what they intended to find into a possible future in each structure they visited. The trick was to see if their visits actually satisfied what their intuitions told them about what they would find on a particular outing.

Each Saturday morning, as they planned an open-house outing for the next day, one of them would try to visualize what he or she thought could be found. One Saturday Mrs. X thought she might want to look for house that had a waterfall on the property. Water had always meant power for that couple, and a waterfall regardless of the particular house would be a powerful image portending a powerful immediate future in that house. Then, after visualizing or intending to look for a property with a waterfall, the couple took down the addresses for their itinerary. They would first go to Beverly Hills, then the canyons, then the Hollywood Hills, and maybe over to Los Feliz before heading home. Or they would go up to the Pacific Palisades or Santa Monica Canyon before taking Sunset east.

These were not pleasurable forays into people's open houses. There was a schedule to keep, real estate agents to fend off, other lookie-loos to deal with, and the general intensity of driving your own life into the lives of others. And always, even though you try not to, you are measuring your own successes against the successes of the people who are either moving up in the world or in trouble, growing and expanding or retrenching. The sellers wouldn't be at the open house. Their real estate agent would have told them to find a place where they could amuse themselves for four and a half hours while the world pored over their belongings and measured their lifestyle as if it were a coat that would fit them.

But into this mix my friends waded, gauging lifestyles and looking for the answer to the question they had posed to themselves the day before. And, like magic, the answers began to come. High up in the hills above Sunset where the twisting roads winding up the side of the Santa Monica mountains become so narrow they are Hummer unfriendly, my friends spotted an open house—not on their list—that sported what looked like a titanium gate shining in the afternoon sun. They found a place to park, no mean feat in the hills above Sunset Plaza, and slid inside the massive gate. Instead of the interior of a house, they found steps to a plateau with two separate structures on either side. The plateau had a magnificent view of the city below, from the Pacific all the way to downtown skyscraper buildings. The scene was like an animated Google map.

From the plateau they walked up to a higher level where they found a lap pool fed by an ever-flowing waterfall. One of the structures was a one-bedroom house with a built-in hot tub in the bedroom itself. Luxury? Yes, but the hot tub was part of the bedroom floor. Try stumbling around in the dark to find the bathroom when you've just roused yourself out of a hellish nightmare and take two steps into a tub of tepid water up to your waist. It was, by definition, a pitfall. So they found their waterfall, just as they had intended, but it came attached to such a dangerous feature that it told them all they needed to know about what a waterfall feature portended, at least on that trip.

On other open-house Sundays, my friends found the pink bedroom they had imagined, a house set in what could almost have been an enchanted forest in one of the Westside canyons and two houses that were actually built over streams. Anything with water running through it in Los Angeles, especially when it's not raining, is such an anomaly that it's kind of like finding the legendary white buffalo. But on this particular Sunday, my friends found one house built over a stream and another house where a stream meandered through the front yard. The point is they were looking for a small water feature and found it even though these were not mentioned in the open-house ads. Their intuition about what they would come across and what it might mean was working. They projected what they were looking for onto real-world events and they beat the law of averages. You can do this, too.

THE INTUITION ON THE OPPOSITE SIDE OF YOUR BRAIN

Here's another series of exercises that will help you tune in to your intuition. Actually, it's designed to show you that your intuition cable is always playing. You only have to tune it in by tuning out the rest of the world to get the signal. Before we go into the principle behind it, just do it. Take a paper and pencil and give yourself lots of room to write. Put the pencil down and begin asking yourself questions out loud, one at a time, before writing down the answer. Ask about your future, your love life, your fondest desires. Ask specific questions for which you can provide specific answers. Then, after each question, pick up the pencil with your opposite hand—your left hand if you're a righty and your right if you're a lefty—and write down the answers. Look at what your opposite hand, freed from the constraints of the logical side of your brain, is telling you. But this is only the beginning.

Next, hold the pencil *in* your opposite hand over the paper. Now with pencil poised above the paper, ask yourself a question out loud, this time a substantive, meaningful question, that can be answered in a sentence or two. The difference here is that the other side of your brain, the nonlogical side, will be the brain asking all the questions. Don't censor them, let your nonlogical brain do all the talking. Now, without thinking about it too much, write out the answer to each question. Keep doing this, asking yourself more and more meaningful questions requiring more insightful answers for the next hour or so.

Above all, regardless of the nonsense that you see on paper, don't analyze yourself. Don't tell yourself that what you're writing is stupid or that it makes you afraid. Just let it flow. Let your voice speak the question and let your opposite hand write down the answers. What you will probably find as you answer the questions is that your answers are coming from a different part of you. They are not the standard answers you get when you think about things. The most revealing answers are the ones that you don't concentrate on but those that come as you concentrate on holding the pen or pencil.

I know that one of the most revealing things about this exercise is that the answers will be completely honest. Only the logical brain can lie. The nonlogical brain that governs your opposite hand can never lie because dissembling is a logical and cultural function. Therefore, ask yourself what you really want, really feel, and really believe. The answers you will get are what you really want, really feel, and really believe. Your heart will be speaking and your intuition about who you are and what you will become is already in place.

THE FINAL INTUITION TEST

Now that you have learned how to recite your mantra, accept your always-flowing intuition signal, and spoken to yourself from the heart, it's time to let your intuition loose to see what it can do. And it's time to jettison any fears you have about nonlogic or looking crazy in the eyes of others. It's time to test out how your intuition makes you feel about the events you encounter.

Here's how the exercise works. It's very simple, but in order to get to it you have to let go of your doubt over your analysis and, above all, your logic. Call it an intuition test, or a test of gut instinct, which is actually another name for intuition. This is another one of those situations you can't force, but have to let happen. Nevertheless, you must begin it by saying your mantra and meditating so that the conscious thoughts of the day that can affect the way you process passive information simply float away and have as little residual effect as possible.

After you have said your mantra and have put yourself into a neutral meditative state, imagine a situation that you are about to enter. It might be a business meeting, a social date, buying a house, renting an apartment, or anything else of consequence. See yourself in that event just like the life-space exercise we talked about earlier. Only in this exercise try not to force yourself to imagine an outcome. Just picture the situation as a space around you. Now try to imagine what you're feeling in the situation. What are your emotions? What are you feeling in your gut? Don't try to explain or rationalize your feelings, simply note them honestly. Now, completely walk yourself through the situation and note all the feelings you have as you come out the other side. Write down the entire experience simply to memorialize it on paper. You're not committing yourself to anything, only capturing your feelings just like you captured your feelings about your dreams.

When you've completed the exercise, go back and read your notes. Next, again without trying to explain anything away, take your pen or pencil in your opposite hand and quiz yourself with meaningful questions about what you wrote and the emotions you experienced in your situational space experience. What is the opposite side of your brain telling you to ask and what are the answers? The combination of your notes and your questions and answers will be very interesting because they will reveal the pure intuition signal that you're receiving and that you might be burying under a ton of logic and rational explanations.

First of all, your gut instinct during the situational space exercise was the most accurate reading or gauge of your emotions. It reveals not something that will definitely turn out one way or another but how you believe or feel something might turn out. Even if your scale was as simple as feel good/feel bad with nothing in between and no gradations, it's telling you a lot. In a job situation, if you're feeling very sick about what you're doing to yourself in a particular meeting, it's your intuition speaking to you about what's really going on. It doesn't mean you can avoid the situation, but it does help you recognize your feelings and the potential for problems on the horizon. Just that recognition will help you through it because many of our problems with life situations happen as a result of our denying the reality and telling ourselves that anything negative that happens is our own stupid fault.

Where this situation space exercise really works is in its ability to help you identify emotions and physical sensations associated with the specific situations. You're considering renting an apartment, walking through the neighborhood, meeting people in elevators, and seeing how you fit. Sure it might be a great apartment at a great price, but is it great if you're going to be unhappy there? Thus, even as you're considering it, you close your eyes, repeat your mantra, cleanse your mind of a logical overlay, and then float your consciousness to the apartment. You visualize yourself there, going up and down in the elevator and meeting people. You see what emotions and physical sensations it evokes. If the sensations and emotions are decidedly negative, realize that it is your intuition speaking to you. Don't deny it, deal with it as the lightning rod it is.

Maybe the skeptics reading this will argue that this entire exercise is only an exercise in subjectivity. There is no objective reality to this, only a measurement of one's own feelings. I agree. However, the point of this exercise in intuition is subjectivity. You learn, by imagining yourself in a variety of life-changing or otherwise significant circumstances, what the effect of those circumstances might well be by experiencing in advance the emotions surrounding or resulting from those circumstances. When you discover how you might feel after having walked through an upcoming event, you should be able to sense whether you need to be there, whether you can avoid being there, or whether you sense danger on the rise.

We're talking about your gut instinct here. When you imagine yourself in a specific situation, you will most likely experience actual physical sensations. It's these sensations that are the key to your emotions. But you feel them often in the pit of your stomach, especially when the image of a future situation gives you the fight or flight reaction that we're all familiar with. Shafica once told me that the explanation for a gut instinct is simple and probably has nothing to do with anything paranormal or extrasensory. She told me way back in the 1960s, one time when I had an overly nervous feeling in the pit of my stomach, that human beings have a nexus of neurons in an area around the stomach, brain cells, that is, right around our stomachs. I pictured it as having two brains, one inside the skull and the other inside the belly. And she said that was right.

Therefore, if Shafica was right back then, when you have that awful sensation of foreboding and it hits you right in the gut, listen to it. It's your intuition talking. Don't dismiss it. Heed it. Don't call yourself a nervous Nellie and walk right into a trap you could have avoided. And don't deny the legitimate feelings you have about people and situations that you probably experience every day of your life. Learn how to say your mantra to open up your communication with the universe, let your doubts and fears float away on the river, and when you have quieted the static that blots out your ability to receive a pure signal of perception from the larger universe, you will experience the absolute fulfillment of hearing your intuition talk to you and guide you through life's situations. You will know, firsthand, that there is much, much more to existence than daily routines, three meals a day and a late-night snack, and the sensations of the world that floods our physical senses. Just imagine the possibilities of being able to experience different types of sensations from your own future, of being able to wield a power of cognition that acts like a radar beam showing you a glide path through life, and of having the confidence to make decisions about yourself based on a real knowledge of what lies in store.

For most people this is only a dream. But for those who know how to tune in and drop out the static, guiding yourself by your intuition is akin to walking along the path of the warrior. Carlos Castaneda in *Conversations with Don Juan,* talks about the alternate reality inhabited by the Yaqui shamans, and Dr. Wayne Dyer talks about this in *Power of Intention, Getting in the Gap,* and *Meditations for Manifesting,* where Dr. Dyer, a guest on *Coast to Coast,* explains how his readers can get the life they truly want through meditation and a discovery and focus of their real intentions.

What I hope you will see from your experiences with meditation and tuning in to your intuition is that there is an actual science behind this. Call it New Age, but that's only a label that limits the power of the experience that lies ahead. In reality, what you will discover is your own hidden brain that's always on and working, but which those who would control the way you lead your life hope you will never discover. What's the nature of the science that lies behind your untapped powers? No less than the science that has already shown that you can psychically project yourself to remote locations, including the future: that you can levitate your own body, as I once did: and that through the sheer power of focusing your intentions, you can actually manipulate the future.

WORKING THE MATRIX:
THE RANDOM
INTUITION EXERCISE

I get a call from someone in the Midwest tonight. It's sleeting in western Missouri where a lonely listener is remembering Christmases past, or, he says, trying to remember.

"Hi George, Merry Christmas," he begins. "I'm pretty much alone tonight so I thought I'd ask you guys a question."

"What's the question?" After years of being on the air, you sometimes can tell a person's age from the sound of their voice. I can almost visualize him just from the cracking in his voice and the effort he's making to keep his volume up. Besides, my own intuition, from practicing what I preach about lucid dreaming and refining one's intuition through these exercises, also teaches how to deal with people. Many times a night, just from the way people ask a question, I can tell what's really bothering them and what they need. Intuition will teach you that as well.

My caller continues, "You're all talking about having a mantra and saying it three times a day or some such. But what if you can't bring it to mind? I have a problem with that. Senior moments." My caller is a victim of television programming, the creation of problems so that specific products can remedy them. Now I do commercials every night. Commercials keep me on the air. Advertising is the lifeblood of radio, television, newspapers, and magazines. But, many times you can also see right behind the advertising to the obvious manipulation. Just watch the television evening news, you know, the news just after dinner, and count the number of digestion aids and prescription drugs for all the ailments that come from watching the television news.

Back to my caller.

"Senior moments are just an advertising label," I tell him. "There's no such thing as a senior moment."

In fact, I tell my caller, there is no such thing as forgetting, really, because everything is stored in his mind, like a recording tape, from the very beginning. Maybe my caller has a problem with spot recall, trying to pinpoint where in his mind that memory lies. But, as Shafica determined for herself fifty years ago when she visited Wilder Penfield in Canada, all memories, all images, and the emotions associated with them are stored in a person's mind.

I tell my caller what I would tell anyone about recall. Disregard anyone who says that it's impossible to recall events of the past, that you're either too overworked or old or feeble to remember the events of things past, because you're not. I have a list of what I call "thoughts to avoid" or cop-outs, which include, near the top, "senior moment." Don't give yourself the excuse that you "never remember things" or that you're losing things from your memory. These are all indicators that part of you simply wants to close shop and go on a cerebral vacation. You're the one creating the leaks in your memory and you're the one with ability to plug them and keep the thoughts flowing. To accomplish this, you have to focus on the positive.

If you can develop a complete confidence in your ability to keep all things in your head at the same time, even if you have to have a mnemonic path to get to them, think of the personal power you will wield. I don't mean that you have to walk around with your address book in the forefront of your recall, but you certainly can carry something around with you on paper, or on your PDA or cell phone. Bolster your ability to keep things current in your mind by relying on whatever resources you can muster. Don't be self-conscious about carrying around a small notepad with key numbers, dates, and names in it. After all, look at what an old spiral-bound did for Detective Columbo when he had to solve a who-dunnit on television.

The key is to assume that you have the ability to remember what you need to remember and not to give yourself excuses for why you may not remember something. You can do this by simply telling yourself to banish all negative thoughts about yourself from your mind. How can you do this? You catch them at the start by realizing that negative thoughts or assumptions about your abilities start inside you. It's your own voice, even disguised as the voice of another, that's carrying the negative message. So whether it's a parent, a toxic friend, your always critical supervisor at work, or a scolding relative, try to screen the message, extracting the personality from the content, and let it float away as if it were spiritual poison. You can always listen to rational criticism when necessary, but self-criticism is simply unnecessary and inhibits your ability to pursue personal empowerment. So don't let others get inside your head where their voices can mask your own fears and doubts about yourself. It's a form of spiritual possession.

Therefore, you must throw out the lesser voices when you feel stymied and sense that you are losing power. If the impression of powerlessness grows and you feel overwhelmed by negative voices or if you find yourself tripping up your own abilities through minor accidents or what others might call "happenstances," plan on doing a "life step-away" where you put yourself, as much as you can, into a state of suspended animation. Try to walk through events as much as you can. Act and pretend that you're invisible and avoid interacting with things as much as possible. Go to work and do your job, of course, but try to distance yourself emotionally from things because you are pulling back to assess them. Keep up your meditation and try to talk to the Big Power while avoiding the little powers over your life. And at the same time, think of looking for signposts in your life.

Just as you do when you discard negative thoughts that intrude on your meditation sessions, discard the self-criticism that comes in the form of voices around you. Let it float away. Picture it like feathers being blown away on a gentle afternoon breeze. You don't hear it. You don't react to it. Let it all pass until there is only silence. And in the silence, all that remains is your mantra and your connection with the universe.

It is in the silence of your connection with the universe that you can walk the matrix and experience the joy of the wholeness of all creation. This, just by itself, is an empowering feeling because it informs you of the majesty of existence, a purpose you can discern for yourself, and the understanding that although you are a unique creature, you are linked to all other creatures regardless of time and place.

If you're in the flow, silently moving through the matrix via your meditative connection, you are likely to experiences flashes of intuition when you imagine yourself in upcoming situations. Just being in the flow will automatically make you receptive to events from the future as impressions flood your awareness. Sometimes these images have no connection to your current reality, and your immediate reaction might be to dismiss them as meaningless flights of fancy. However, just like daydreaming, these images do have a purpose and might even be portents of future possibilities because being in the flow puts you into a state of timelessness.

A friend of mine told me this story, and it makes sense to me. Once, when he was a new hire at a company, he set his eyes on a position there that he really wanted. Although processing paperwork in his cubicle from nine to five and with no real angle on getting into a supervisory slot, my friend could only hope for a break. Each night, as he repeated his mantra to himself before going off to sleep, he let the vicissitudes of the day pass through him, not lingering on the cubicle skirmishes that marked the company and often overflowed to the coffee machine and microwave oven.

Over the ensuing months, he learned to disengage from the daily grind, do his job, and become more of a presence by his silence than by his aggression. While he was doing this, he began to fantasize, he thought, or daydream. As he recited his mantra, he thought he could hear voices talking to him. He didn't dismiss these sensations out of hand. Rather, he listened, not denying whatever it was that was coursing through his mind.

Sure enough, it was one of the managers talking to him. He was sitting at his desk in the cubicle on a very routine day, reviewing insurance claims to make sure they were signed and had the supporting documentation before labeling them and sending them up the line. His phone rang, which it almost never did unless one of the supervisors' assistants was on the other end, chewing him out for a missed signature or an incorrect claim label ID number.

But in his mantra-induced fantasy, or so he thought, it was one of the managers from human resources on the other end of the line. A supervisory position had opened up in his department and, because his file processing had been so error-free, he clearly knew what he was doing and would be more effective as a supervisor overseeing the work of others. Could he go upstairs for an interview?

In his rational mind, my friend dismissed the voice. Nobody even knew he existed at the company. It was wishful thinking. He would indulge it, of course. It kept him going in the darkness of his apartment. But he wouldn't invest any hope in it because, after all, it was only a dream.

The fantasy kept creeping into his mind for months, sometimes even when he was at work. He would stare at the phone on his desk, almost thinking it was about to ring. He knew, or thought he knew, exactly what a manager's voice on the other end of the line would sound like even though he had rarely spoken to one of the managers. His pay grade was too low and worker bees rarely spoke to bosses that high up in the company. Yet, during the day and at night, the fantasy visions continued.

You might think these were disturbing visions because they were all thought and no action. But they weren't. On the contrary, they were quite pleasant because my friend felt he was transported into a different future, to a place where someone in the faceless pantheon of lawyers and bosses on the upper floors recognized him because of his work and wanted to beam him up. It was a happy thought, but he had no false illusions about its ever happening.

My friend lived and worked in Seattle. If you've never been to Seattle, especially in December or January, you have no idea what it's like to travel to work in the morning darkness. And I mean darkness, even at eight-thirty. And there's the incessant rain. Sometimes it rains in sheets, but other times, the rain is a penetrating perpetual sprinkle. Rain, carried on the teeth of a raw wind, not freezing, but darn cold, works its way through whatever you're wearing and chills you to the skin. By the time you've made your way through the darkness and fog to the office, you're happy just to stand under one of the hot-air grates in the ceiling and wait for the heat to drive away the chill.

It was on one of these rainy, dark, December mornings when, if you didn't know any better, you'd think the sun was dying in the sky and the world was near its end, that my friend reached his cubicle to hear his phone ringing. Why was the phone ringing this early? Nobody ever called him before lunch. But, he had a funny feeling, as if there was a glow around the phone, so he suppressed an instinct to let the call roll over to voice mail while he stood there to dry off. Tracking water across his cubicle carpet, and no doubt incurring a possible glowering look from one of the office supervisors who regularly came by to make sure workers weren't goofing off inside their cubicles, my friend made it to the phone in time and picked up the receiver.

"Good morning," the voice said authoritatively at the other end, as if the caller knew it was a good morning despite the saturating rain and the eerie darkness. But there was also something else about this call that brought my friend sharply to attention. He knew the voice without knowing the voice, knew what it would say next because he had heard it before.

"This is Human Resources. Managers up in claims have been looking over your work," the voice said. "They see all the claims forms come in through screening before they're processed and we've seen how you highlighted the missing information and the errors. Saved them an enormous amount of time. They want you to supervise the work down there. In fact, a slot has opened up for a junior supervisor and we want you to come up here to interview for it. Can you come in at ten?"

My friend barely managed to stammer out his "Okay." Of course there was a moment of shock, a shock anyone might have felt had that person heard this message in his or her own fantasy vision and then heard it again in reality. But, the shock wore off in seconds. In its place was an overwhelming feeling of completeness, a feeling that what my friend had experienced was a connection, across time and space, to the entire universe. He was at one with all creation, not because he was about to get a job that he had been wishing for, but because he had heard this, imagined this moment, word for word, in his own mind and now was experiencing it in reality.

To this day my friend has no explanation. If you're looking for a testable scientifically quantifiable explanation, neither do I. All he knows is that the event, which intruded itself into his imagination during his meditative thinking as if it were a radio broadcast, finally took place months later exactly as he had perceived it. And all I know is that I've heard so many other stories like this one from my callers and listeners that it has become almost second nature to me. If you were to come up to me on the street to tell me that at times you've actually predicted the future, I would be more likely to agree with you than not because I have heard this before.

This anecdote really goes to show that there is a link between what we call intuition and the ability to foresee events in the future. Your intuition cannot only tell you what may be coming your way but what to avoid or in what direction to head. In this case, my friend's intuition told him to pick up that phone regardless of how wet he was even though he had no specific idea that the impressions he was receiving during his private meditative sessions were actually portents of his own future. And they played out exactly as he heard them in his own mind.

Another friend of mine has a son that told me a very interesting story about how to interpret intuitive events. My friend's youngest son was out of college and looking to break into the independent film industry. Meanwhile, he was doing off-and-on production assistant jobs in television and figuring out the best ways to use his skills. However, he wasn't really sure what his skills were and wasn't that confident that he had any. But he kept on writing short scripts for independent movies in the hopes that he could find a way to get one of them made. One short script he wanted to write, but ultimately never did, was a story about a bunch of friends who wire up the glove compartment of their car as a refrigerator, take off for the California desert, and, in a final scene out amid the scrub and chaparral on a brutally hot summer day, feast on ice-cold sushi from the car's refrigerator. I'm not doing his story justice, I know.

My friend's son told his father and a few of his own friends about the story, but other than that, did nothing with it. His father said that he should hit the advertising agency that represented Volkswagen because rather than a short independent movie, his script really deserved to be made into a commercial for the car company. But, again, he did not approach VW or its ad agency with the idea. And a few years passed.

Then, just last year, he turned on his TV to watch a ballgame when, lo and behold, he was transfixed by a very familiar story. The commercial opened with a shot through the windshield of a road through the desert, sand and scrub brush flew by as a huge intense setting sun hung directly over the horizon. A hand reached down into the glove compartment, which opened to a smoky frost, icy even. The hand reached into the glove compartment and pulled out a package of obviously very cold sushi. Even the wrapping on the sushi had a thin coating of ice over the top as the condensation of icy air smoked out into the camera.

"Volkswagen," the voice said. And at this point my friend's son was out of his chair, screaming at the ceiling and whoop-whooping at what he had just seen.

You might think that he was screaming for the first lawyer he could find to sue whomever had put together that commercial, stolen his idea. You might think that he was furious at himself, near frantic that he had shot his mouth off about his idea so as to put it into the ether for someone else to snag and make a profit off it. But these weren't at all his thoughts at that moment. And what he did think is instructive for all of us.

I actually talked to him about it, and his explanation was not just rational and mature, it was thoroughly self-sustaining. He explained that his reaction that night on seeing his idea on the screen was one of pure joy and exhilaration. Of course, he would have liked to have been the writer who presented that commercial to Volkswagen. Who wouldn't? Nevertheless, it was still his idea and the fact that someone else independently came up with it, sold it to Volkswagen, and produced it absolutely thrilled him. It meant that he was right. He was on track. He had what it takes. He came up with an idea that was not only workable, it was bankable. And because he had come up with it, he would come up with other ideas that were just as good and he would sell them. In fact, my friend's son, far from becoming demoralized at seeing his idea on the screen, was liberated. He knew whatever job he took to keep the lights on was just a job while he pursued his own career as a filmmaker. Whether it was for commercials or for the big opening at Sundance, it didn't matter. My friend's son had found his métier and he would pursue it.

The implications of events like these, and my friend's experience is not the only one I've heard along that line, are potentially vast. What if intuition or the ability to perceive events from your own future are not just the province of those gifted enough to be called "psychic"? What if each and every one of us possesses this exact same ability, in varying degrees, so that simply by training oneself through a series of easy-to-master exercises, each of us can tune in the signal carrying the messages of our own futures? If that's the case, and I believe it is, here are some simple exercises you can use to stretch your own innate abilities to foretell events in the future and plan your actions accordingly. I call it looking for signs.

Here's an obvious one, but it's indicative of the thought process. Let's say that you have important personal messages to deliver, phone calls to make. Maybe you're applying for a new job. Maybe you have to make a painful phone call on a personal matter, but you're conflicted about it. Nevertheless, you try to make the call. However, every time you try, you get interrupted. You get busy signals instead of the answering machine. You dial the number but the phone waits and waits before you can hear the ringing at the other end. You get the timed-out message. The answering machine at the other end picks up but then drops the call before you can leave your message. You try on your cell phone, but keep getting a "call failed" message. Whatever it is, intuitively or instinctively you realize that something is in the way of that call and you might have to use Herculean efforts to get that call through. Instead of using those efforts, take it as a sign that this will be a negative thing and maybe you should forego the call at least for the time being. Realize that at least for the immediate present, you can't get there from here and you should delay the trip until the negative clouds part and you can get through. It's not admitting defeat, it's acknowledging that you've picked up a sign that this is not the right time to send that message. This is what I mean by looking for a sign.

Here are some quick decision-making exercises to use when you're conflicted. Regardless of the nature of the decision you have to make, you find yourself asking whether this one is a "yes" or "no." Even with qualifications, this is a pretty basic go or no-go decision. Maybe you have an instinct you're not listening to. Maybe you're fighting yourself over the decision. Whatever it is, you need something a little more definite than a coin toss to figure out which way you should go. How do you decide? Open up the yellow pages at random. Either close your eyes and open them or run your finger through the pages without your looking and open at the page you come to. On that page you will see an image that you will be able to interpret as your answer. You can stop there and go with what you interpret to be the direction you should take or, if you want to refine it, do this a few more times. On the average, you will come across an array of images that will help you make your decision. It's an exercise in interpretation, which can be very fruitful.

As another exercise, put the decision you need to make in the back of your mind. Now, plop down in front of a TV, take the remote control, and, without any predetermined pattern, start flipping from channel to channel. Go through all the channels keeping your mind open. You'll go through the Spanish language stations, the Korean stations, the Japanese stations, the retro channels, the networks, sports channels. Keep going. As you land on each channel, let the images you see talk to you. If you see negative images, then your decision is a no. If you see positive images, then your decision is a yes. How many no's do you get? How many times to you land on a yes? You'll figure out your direction pretty quickly.

Don't want to try the TV exercise? Then get out of the house and take a walk. Open your mind not to interact with what you encounter but to take in the images and see how they hit you. Take a walk downtown. Take a walk through your neighborhood. Take a walk through the woods or along the beach. It doesn't matter where as long as you walk through a place where you can see images that will impact on your thoughts. Does what you encounter tell you to keep going forward in the same direction, or does it tell you to change direction? Do you see patterns of your life in the things you encounter, or do you see things that seem to contradict the patterns in your life? Look at the street signs you pass. What do they say? Are there new meanings in the same old signs and street names? Look at traffic lights. Are there more greens than reds, more yellows than greens? Don't try to overanalyze what you see, go only with the impressions you get from the things you encounter.

You might ask yourself as well, what kinds of decisions are you making. Are you wrestling over big decisions in your life? Can your meditative state and your communication with the Big Power of the universe help you find the paths that will lead you to the big decisions? If so, then you're probably in the flow. You are working on your decisions. However, if you find yourself chasing small things all the time, and only you can determine what is a big decision and what is a small one, then either you are avoiding the big decisions or you're happy chasing the small decisions. Ask yourself whether you are happy with minor decisions or whether your actions are simply avoidance behaviors. Here's one test. Honestly confront yourself about whether you are satisfied with the decisions you are making or whether you are settling for the decisions you are making. If the latter, then maybe what you're doing is simply rearranging the deck chairs on the *Titanic* rather than looking out for icebergs.

Maybe, if you're stuck in a rut going around in a circle with your life, you can use your intuition and innate ability to sense the future to get you out of it. You can do this, just like you've done the previous exercises in this chapter, by looking for a random seed generator somewhere and using it to bounce off into the matrix to find your future there. Throw your decisions up in the air to see how things look when you don't put spins on them. In a variation on the yellow pages exercise, try doing a random image exercise on the Internet.

Get on the Internet and pull up the Google search engine. Then, if you've got a decision to make or simply want to explore some options, pick a key word you're deciding about: *job, house, spouse, child, car, Buick, money, Tucson, Mauritius,* or just about anything. Type in the word and hit return, letting the Google search engine find the sites it associates with your key word. You will see a list of sites, probably thousands of sites stretching across many hundreds of pages. Without exercising too much thought, pick any site at random and click on it. What comes up? Whatever it is, try to associate that site with your decision. Now interpret what you see. Pick another site, and click on it. What do you see? Do this over and over a few times and you will begin to see an image of how your decision might lay itself out. The more key words you select and the more sites you visit and interpret, will ultimately guide you toward your decision.

How is this like remote viewing? In a way it's very much like remote viewing because you're using a series of random items as coordinates, similar to the way Ingo Swann and the early remote viewing trainers used random numbers to associate with the targets the viewers were being sent to. Only by your using Google, it's as if the Internet itself is your tasker, feeding you the random number. You're using the randomness of the Google search engine to find a number of sites. Then, your intuition guides you to the sites you click on where you will find some information regarding the destination, your decision.

Another explanation has to do with something called the Akashic Record, the record of all events. You're hitting the random number to lead you to a place where all brains are linked and you are linked via your engrams stored—inscribed is a better word—in the Akashic Record. You see, if you are going to travel to a place where all brains are linked, you will find the links from that place to your brain. You are part of the Akashic Record not only because you're alive, but because you were destined to be alive. Your engrams already preexist you.

Here's another way to reach that great link to find a path to a decision you have to make. Try a site called randomwebsite.com. That engine itself is its own random number generator, bouncing you directly to a site without you having to do anything other than call it up. Give it a shot. Type in *www.randomwebsite.com* and, I suggest, bookmark it. Then when you call it up, the splashpage will say in large type, ran-domlink. Simply click on randomlink and you will be taken to a website, any site. The random number generator has chosen it for you. What's so great about that? Simply this, you can use randomlink as a kind of instant digital tarot card. Ask a ques-tion, detailed or general, whatever you like. When you click on randomlink, what site comes up? Use that site to interpret the answer to the question you asked. Sure it's subjective, but so what? It's a start.

Want to see if there's a pattern? Start with the most general questions. You don't even have to ask them out loud. You may want to write them down, however. Ask a general question and click on randomlink. See what you get. Then, use the links on the site that randomwebsite has chosen for you to take you to other places. What do you find? Was it helpful?

If you hit what you think is a dead end or you've come to the edge of a decision tree, start it all over again. Ask another question, maybe a more detailed one, and hit randomlink. Keep doing this as an exercise whenever you are completely perplexed about what direction to take. If you want to prepare yourself for this, try going to this site after a nice, relaxing, twenty-or thirty-minute meditation session in which you've discarded as many negative or overly analytical thoughts as you can. Then, when you approach randomlink, you may be more open to the kinds of images you will see.

Give these exercises a try and you will see that by opening your mind up to possibilities and by not being afraid to chal-lenge logical or conventional reason, you will see directions you never realized existed. At the same time, you will be empower-ing yourself. You will be allowing yourself to experience the power of the universe that you're always connected to, but sometimes need help in interpreting. You will find that you are a repository of power, a member of a great link of shared knowledge. And you have the ability to partake of that knowledge and to use that link as a kind of psychic superhighway to travel into your own future.

Rick from Kentucky

Then there was Rick from Kentucky, who called to say that the night reminded him of the time he saw a demon staring into his window when he was a young boy. He said the creature had a round bloody face, no neck or shoulders, and eyes rolled back into his head so he could see only the whites. Although he drives the interstates and country routes at night, to this day he stays away from windows at night, never knowing if that demon will visit him again. By the sound of his voice and the stress he was under, I could tell that whether real, a dream, or a momentary flicker of light on an otherwise dark night, Rick absolutely believed what he was saying. If that creature is real, it's still out there. So my intuition tells me.

EXERCISES IN POSITIVE PROJECTION AND FOCUSED CONSCIOUSNESS

H ey, George," another caller asks on the "West of the Rockies" line. "You ever going to do another one of those group prayers for when the asteroid hits us?"

"What asteroid?" I ask him. "Is this a new asteroid? How did I miss it?"

The night is wearing on and the rain is getting heavier. I'm going to take it really easy on the roads.

"No," he says. "Same asteroid that always can hit us. Just wondering about if you can move the asteroid out of the way with one of those focused prayers like you moved the hurricane. You know, do with your mind what those astronauts want to do with a space ship and the asteroid."

I understand him now. A few years ago, we were engaged in what I was calling focused prayer, a group concentration of consciousness, directed, like a psychic particle beam weapon, at a single event or object. The target back then was a hurricane. The weather forecasters had said that the hurricane barreling through the Gulf of Mexico, headed for New Orleans, was a whopper. It was becoming a category four and maybe even a category five. The levees, the engineers were saying, wouldn't be able to hold back the storm surge, the flood of water like a tidal wave that would overwhelm the bulwarks and send Lake Pontchartrain surging into downtown New Orleans. No, this wasn't Hurricane Katrina in 2005. It was a few years earlier.

But the stakes were just as high as this storm made its way north across the Gulf to bear down on Louisiana.

As the storm gathered strength, weather forecasters and hurricane center commentators posted dire predictions for the Crescent City. They knew that a massive storm surge over twenty feet would swamp the levees and that wind-driven waves would push water from the lake into the downtown area. Army Engineers also knew that once the levees were breached and water flooded the pumping stations, the city wouldn't be able to force water out of the streets. In short, New Orleans, which easily flooded even during regular rainstorms, would be inundated.

That night, as the hurricane followed its warm-water path to the Louisiana coast, I asked my audience, wherever they were in the world, to pray with me, to focus their minds on an image of the storm. It didn't matter whether they knew what a hurricane looked like from satellite imagery or whether they'd only seen pictures of storms on television. All I asked my audience participants to do was to think about a storm in the Gulf of Mexico making its way toward Louisiana. They didn't even have to know what Louisiana looked like or where the Gulf of Mexico was, although most of my audience knew exactly what they had to imagine when they were sending their energy out there.

Through the night, from phone calls and Internet "fast blasts," the instant e-mail messages audience members sent me via our *Coast* website, I knew that people were gathering. I had talked about this focused prayer endeavor the day before when it became clear from the storm track that the hurricane would hit New Orleans. And the night that the storm was due to make landfall, I asked my audience, those who wanted to participate, to focus all their prayers and spiritual energies on dissipating the eye of the storm so as to weaken it and to turn the track of the storm away from New Orleans.

Other people had warned me not to engage in this type of exercise. They said that trying to fine-tune the energies of millions of people toward a single effect would at its most benign be a fruitless endeavor because nothing would happen. It would be like Geraldo breaking open Al Capone's safe on live television only to find that nothing was in there. And that was at its most benign. At worst, some critics said, it would be like Dr. Frankenstein tampering with the forces of nature. "You don't know what you could be unleashing," they said.

Yet, one had only to look at the radar imagery of the approaching storm, the hugeness of its wind and rain areas as it stretched across the Gulf, the fiery orange of its wind intensity around the eye, to know that New Orleans would be helpless against the onslaught. Even back then it was no surprise that the levees would give. Engineers had said that in a category five hurricane, the levees would not be able to hold back the storm surge and that once the levees were breached and the power went out in the city, the pumps would not be able to flush the water out of the streets. In fact, even back then it was almost an accepted fact that in a violent hurricane, New Orleans, which had historically been protected by a stretch of wetlands, now gone, could be almost wiped out. So for me, assessing the possibilities, it was worth the chance to save a city, see if the power of focused prayer worked, and mobilize millions of people to exert a force for good in the world.

And so, on the radio, through the night, I exhorted my listeners who wanted to participate to focus their mental energies on that storm. I suggested that in their prayers they imagine that they could weaken it, deprive it of energy from the warm water beneath it, disturb the eye wall of the storm so that its winds would diminish. I also suggested to members of our focused prayer audience to concentrate on diverting the storm's direction. Just a few degrees of deviation, say to the east, would spare New Orleans a direct hit. The storm surge might not be as high and the winds would not be as destructive.

As we waited through the hours of darkness, hurricane warning reports gradually began filtering in. The storm drew closer to land and, then, miraculously, the storm seemed to be losing intensity. Just as miraculously, the storm seemed to be veering away, ever so slightly, from a direct-hit path to New Orleans. My audience prayed harder, focused their own energies more intensely, and their efforts were paying off. As a dark gray dawn broke over the southeast, it was clear, to me at least, that our prayers had worked because the hurricane had weakened and had been diverted from a direct hit on the city.

How did I know that the prayers had worked? Just because a few million people had concentrated their energies on a single focal point and the event changed, why should I assume that a *post hoc* was a *propter hoc,* as my old freshman English professor once lectured? It is a fallacy that just because one event (A) follows another event (B) to assume that A caused B. In the case of the hurricane, however, I do believe that the concentrated force of millions of wills is enough to effect a change in a natural occurrence. First, the concentration is a focus for good rather than for evil. If good is light and evil is pitch-blackness, then just the single flicker of a flame on a darkest night is enough to give light to those around it, something our prehistoric ancestors in caves certainly understood. Therefore, the force of good will always overcome forces of chaos and destruction.

Second, scientific experiments have shown that individuals are capable, when they can turn off their analytical overlay, to effect changes in physical events. There have been at least two scientific experiments that have shown this. The first, as the Princeton Engineering Anomalies Research (PEAR) project demonstrated, to state it simplistically, individuals could control physical events in the real world through concentration on the event. Dr. Morris Freedman at the University of Toronto, however, found the PEAR study lacking in some scientific bases, and sought to duplicate it using subjects with frontal lobe damage against a control group of subjects with normal brain functionality. And Dr. Freedman found there was a statistical difference between his two groups, indicating to him, as he wrote in the *Journal of Scientific Exploration*, vol. 17, no. 4, pp. 651–668, 2003, that individuals probably had some power, if they could minimize their self-awareness, to impose what he calls "intentionality" on physical events in the real world. Let's put this into everyday-eese. It means, again oversimplifying, that if a person can somehow reduce her awareness of herself to something close to zero, she can use her will to create a physical effect that has not yet occurred—influence the future—in the real world. Scientifically measured, scientifically reproducible.

Perhaps the most profound example of global consciousness and its interactions with physical events seemingly beyond its control is the Egg Project at PEAR back in 2001. The Egg Project creators wrote that they wanted to see whether there was any correlation, in their words, "anomalous interaction between the real world and human consciousness as measured globally." They wrote on their website (http://noosphere.prince ton.edu/terror.html) that they were looking for evidence of a "developing global consciousness that might react to events with deep meaning." And they found it.

They set up the experiment by placing random number generator packages in computers owned and operated by volunteers around the world. The random number generators, called "EGGS" sent their random numbers back to a server in Princeton at fifteen-minute intervals. The point here was to gather enough random number data from different points around the world to be analyzed at a single server to see if any patterns in the random numbers emerged so as to indicate they were being influenced by something. Could human events, physical events in the real world as they were perceived by human beings, influence the pattern of numbers from different sites around the globe? And if events could influence the seemingly independent random number generators, was there a kind of global consciousness that could be reflected in the behavior of the random computers?

Evidence of that relationship between a global consciousness and a real world event came on September 11, 2001, when the EGGs around the world were analyzed by the server to show that there was a shift out of the randomness as the terrorist attacks on the World Trade Center played themselves out. It was as if there was somehow a link between human global consciousness, anticipating and then witnessing the event, and the behavior of the seemingly independent computers. For a far more complete analysis of all of this, you can go to the PEAR homepage on the Internet or click directly over to http://noosphere.princeton.edu/terror.html.

For me, this experiment shows that my experiments in focused human consciousness with respect to the hurricane in the Gulf that threatened New Orleans before Katrina have a palpable basis in reality. Human conscious can, in fact, exert some control over events in the real world. Another dramatic example of this took place during the October 2002 Beltway Sniper case in the Washington, D.C. suburbs.

Coming as they did just about a year after 9-11, the unfolding case put America on edge because many people thought that these were terrorist attacks and not the work of a serial killer. When the killer, or someone who identified himself as the killer, began taunting the police, à la Jack the Ripper, the Black Dahlia killer, the Unabomber, the Green River Killer, and Dennis Rader aka BTK, law enforcement officials came to believe that they had a kind of "Freeway Shooter" on their hands rather than an al-Quaeda terrorist. Although the case would take some dramatic turns, that is essentially how it played out.

The shootings began with a round fired through a plate glass window at Michael's Arts and Crafts Store in Aspen Hill, Maryland. Less than an hour later James Martin was killed by a single shot while he stood in a supermarket parking lot in Silver Spring, Maryland. One day later, five victims were each killed with a single shot. Before forty-eight hours had passed, police in the Beltway counties knew they had a serial sniper on their hands, someone mobile enough to drive to a protected location, set up, squeeze off a kill shot, and vanish into the exodus of traffic from D.C. Was this an al-Quaeda operative, or a group of terrorists, wreaking havoc in the neighborhoods surrounding the nation's capital?

Operating on the initial belief that this was a terrorist activity, federal agencies quickly joined a task force to investigate the homicides, resulting in an ad hoc law enforcement group of county sheriffs, state law enforcement, the FBI, and the Bureau of Alcohol, Firearms, and Tobacco. The resulting flood of press releases and profiles fed the fears of an already worried and vulnerable population while the killer himself—who was presumed to be a male—was on the loose.

As profiles of the killer were developed from law enforcement sources and the many serial killer consultants hired by the news organizations covering the unfolding events, the experts began vying with each other for whose profile was the most accurate. The media, heavily concentrated in the Beltway area, played the story up, citing lead after lead. Each new headline prompted witnesses to report that they had seen a suspect vehicle—in many instances a white Chevy van—and local police, already stretched very thin, rushed to the areas. Then, as news channels pressed for interviews with local law enforcement officials, spokespersons in the police command began to divulge more information about their investigation. As most homicide investigators will tell you, this is usually a big mistake because most serial killers, the overwhelming majority of which are control-type offenders, intensively follow the news of their crimes. Therefore, releasing any information about the crime or the killer to the news media is tantamount to telling the killer exactly what the police know. And because only the killer knows the deepest secrets of his crimes, he can figure out where the police are in their investigation. In this case, the news about the white van told the killer that the police were looking for the wrong vehicle, allowing the killer freedom of movement.

Serial killers have told police that they pick up news about themselves from police press conferences. In the Beltway Sniper case, the one-on-one media dialogue between killer and cops became even more obvious when a police official said during an on-air interview that he was glad, at least, that the killer had not targeted any schools. Maybe the killer took that as a public taunt because he quickly set up on the Benjamin Tasker school and wounded a student there. Serial killers have to assert control, control over their victims, and control over the community in which they're committing their crimes. In a spree of shootings across the Beltway suburbs, the killer demonstrated that he could strike at will, that no one was safe on the streets or in public places, and that he was in control of the media and the police. Thus, when a law enforcement official pointed to an area where the killer had not struck, it was an open invitation for the killer to attack. And as if to emphasize that he got the message from the police, the killer left his tarot calling card at the site. That incident alone should have told police to cut off all communication about the killer with the media. But it didn't.

The police opened up a public dialogue with the killer, giving 800 numbers for him to contact them. At the same time, various pundits appeared on a variety of news and talk shows, each one offering his official profile of the killer. Even *The Washington Post* wrote that the problem with all the profiles was not so much that they were probably wrong, but that they were influencing potential witnesses, who were more intent on finding someone who fit the profile than in actually looking around for what they could see. For example, as Dr. Robert Keppel wrote in his textbook *The Psychology of Serial Killer Investigations,* the fact that news organizations and pundits had people looking around for a white Chevy van made them oblivious to an innocuous Chevy Caprice that turned up in a gas station and on ATM surveillance cameras near the crime scenes. The killers might have been able to evade police detection for so long, Keppel writes, because everyone, even the police, were focused on the profiles that didn't even come close to identifying the killers. The police didn't realize that the killer wasn't attacking individual victims because of who they were, he was attacking anyone who was a target of opportunity out in the open.

Ultimately, the choral nature of the news coverage and one-on-one law enforcement interviews was turning the investigation into a circus. Everyone was getting into the act as if catching the Beltway Sniper was tantamount to snagging the first live alien to pop out of a flying saucer before it was whisked away to Area 51. It was descending into chaos. And when one television show host put up his own 800 number for the killer to call him, just in case he didn't want to talk to the police, who were begging him to call, I said to myself that we had had enough.

Having, I believe, successfully conducted a focused prayer group to divert and weaken a hurricane, I decided to conduct a group that would make the invisible killers visible to the police. I had read enough true crime to know that in serial killer investigations, especially long-term ones, police usually have the killer's identity somewhere in their records. Unfortunately, they don't know that they have this information and, therefore, usually overlook it. And I figured it might be the case here as well. Somewhere, somehow, the killers had been on camera, had signed into hotel in the area, had been spotted in a local restaurant or in a parking lot, but that information had not made it into a daily briefing. So we would have to focus on making them stand out.

I asked my audience to pray for the killers to become visible, to pray that someone, somewhere, would come across the killers and alert the police so that they could be stopped. Because serial killers by their very nature are able to hide in plain sight, cloaked by the community in which they troll for victims of opportunity, I asked my audience participants to focus on making the killers stand out, to raise them in a higher relief from their background. And, while investigators were looking all around for that mysterious white van, the killer's car miraculously turned up in plain sight on October 24, 2002, along I-95. A witness reported to police that there were men sleeping in a Chevy Caprice pulled off the road alongside the highway. The car was surrounded by police, the occupants were interrogated, and John Lee Malvo ultimately confessed to being a participant in the shootings.

If you read enough true crime, you will see a pattern to most of the ways invisible serial killers become visible. Often it seems serendipitous. Other times you can tell that it is the police who are making their own luck. In the Beltway Sniper case, police discovered that the killers were transients living out of their car. They could pull off the road, park their car at the end of a lot outside the circle of a streetlight, and sleep until the sun rose. Then they would stop at any convenience store for food, and troll for a victim out in the open and away from any police cars. One of the team would spot for the other, telling him on a two-way radio, if there was any danger in sight. The triggerman would fire a single shot and then the two would pull away while witnesses congregated around the victim. Their nondescript car simply faded into the background even though it was caught on a number of surveillance cameras.

When my audience focused in on making the killers visible, one might not have figured that it would have happened so suddenly. It was literally hours after I had asked my audience to participate that witnesses reported Malvo and Mohammed sleeping in the car alongside the road. I would say it was not serendipity at all but an actual intervention of human consciousness into physical real-world events. It was an example of how focused intentionality can actually change the future, effect events that might be seemingly random, and alter a time-line.

"So you caught the Beltway Snipers?" my caller asks.

"No, all I did was ask my audience to focus on making them visible to police in such a way that their appearance would lead to their discovery."

What we did with our focused consciousness exercises wasn't magic or voodoo. It was ultimately a process in which audience participants were guided to lay aside their individual senses of self-awareness, a consciousness of self, to join a collective consciousness in which individuals were sublimated to a greater mind so that they could focus that collective consciousness to create an intentionality. And here we tread into places where traditional science says we cannot go. The world of Newtonian physics says that real-world events are the result of natural causes, not the psychic intentionality of any human beings. You can't "will" storms to come into being or to dissipate. That's the stuff of the *Twilight Zone* or *Outer Limits*. You can't make something happen.

Yet, what the folks at PEAR discovered was that there is a relationship between human consciousness, albeit on a global scale, and real-world happenings, a relationship that is measurable. What the scientists at the University of Toronto found out was that within a clinical setting, individuals who had the ability to set aside their self-awareness had the ability to effect changes in the real world of physical events. Their intentionality trumped natural happenstance. And what I discovered was that groups of individuals, potentially millions of individuals, acting collectively, had the power to weaken a storm and to divert it from its path. I discovered that invisible merchants of evil, serial snipers, could be illuminated with a psychic light such that after three weeks of invisibility amid the crowd, they suddenly became visible.

The power of this effect was so great that even Art Bell, my predecessor on *Coast to Coast AM* and one of the founders of late-night talk radio on subjects of the paranormal, warned me against doing these exercises. Other friends cautioned me against it, too, arguing that I was tinkering with something that was real and very powerful. It was so powerful, they said, that it was a force that, if not guided carefully, could unleash real havoc in the universe. Their descriptions of the consequences were dire indeed. They said that for every storm you divert from one path, you turn it to another. Imagine sending the storm away from New Orleans but into the very heart of nearby Gulfport. Do you want to be responsible for the destruction you would cause that would otherwise not be caused? It's one of the ultimate conundrums. It opens up the door to the multiverse for sure. How do you contemplate the magnitude of changing the direction of nature? Or, on the other hand, are you simply just another force of nature? You made John Mohammed's Chevy Caprice visible to people driving along the highway. Might it not have become visible all by itself because the two shooters, worn out and on the run from police, who would at some point have checked the surveillance photos from the crime scenes and seen the same car over and over again and have figured that whoever was driving this car was a possible material witness if not the suspect himself? But, one might say, just the fact that millions of people intervened probably saved one or more lives. In which membrane of the multiverse would the people whose lives were saved have influenced the lives of others? You see what happens when you get into the business of unleashing forces with the capacity for changing the future. And we're doing this from the side of good. Imagine what could happen if people honed in on this ability to channel forces for the side of evil.

The channeling of evil was an issue many of my friends raised. They said, imagine this enormous power that you're delivering to people by showing them how to focus their prayers. What would happen if a group assembled, communicated via phones and the Internet, and in so doing managed to focus prayers that were destructive in their intent? Look at what you've demonstrated. You've shown what the sheer application of desire manifested by a group of millions of individuals who lay aside their own individual personas to focus on a single point can effect. You've shown, and this is the big one, that events in the physical world are directly controllable by people's mind. It changes our whole definition of reality, changes the very ways we perceive what we believe to be the world around us. If we can change the future via our thought, affect the ways even forces of nature play out, what does that say about the nature of humanity?

Sure, our desire is to turn this force for the good. But there is no magic mechanism preventing anyone from using this force for evil. Indeed, I can tell you stories that I've heard about people who are the victims of just this kind of focused energy. One friend of mine has complained that he is the subject of some kind of psychic attack by forces within our own government. I cannot verify that what he's saying is true, but it sounds as if he may be the victim of something.

According to what he's told me, he was publishing a book about how cabals within our government operate out of their own self-interest. I'm not going to go into detail about this, but if you use your imagination, you can probably figure out what kind of self-interest he is talking about. Suffice it to say that the nature of the events my friend is referring to have to do with catastrophes, assassinations, and other types of clandestine activities that appear to be the work of others, but are really the work of this group. My friend published a number of books about what has come to be known as the "secret government," elite officials who really call the shots behind the Beltway Curtain, and thereafter, he says, he became a victim of that secret government. Only it wasn't black SUVs that suddenly turned up in his driveway or across the street, and it wasn't the mysterious white unmarked van parked down the block, it was a psychic attack.

What's a psychic attack?

It works like this, my friend told me. First, he had a general feeling of unease as if something were out of kilter in his psyche. He had no physical symptoms per se, but a sense that things were not right. He was bumping into stuff, had a not-quite headache, was generally tired, and couldn't focus his mind on the tasks at hand. He thought he was seriously ill so he went to his doctor. After some serious preventive medical testing, the lab came up with absolutely nothing. No tired blood, no senior moments, no vitamin deficiency anemia, no irregularity, nothing. Then the anxiety started. He was nervous every time the phone rang, almost jumped out of his pajamas when someone was at the door, and was even afraid to go out to the driveway to pick up the morning paper. At the sound of a barking dog, he was at the window looking to see who might be lurking in the bushes. But he saw nothing.

My friend is a rational guy. If he can't see it, it's not there. When I once tried to explain to him that the little gray extra-terrestrials people always talk about have a way to make them-selves vibrate at a certain frequency that allows light to pass through them so they're invisible to all but a trained eye, my friend laughed so hard I thought he would choke. "And you do a radio show about this?" He would roar. And when I told him that I'd read where the presence of these small gray aliens is sometimes indicated by a faint pungent smell, like cinnamon or cloves, he just about doubled up. "And I suppose they talk to you," he also said.

"Not really 'talk,'" I once explained. "They kind of click the way dolphins do," and directed him to read some of the books by Courtney Brown on the nature of extraterrestrials. That, too, set him off on peals of laughter.

Therefore, it was astonishing to me when he reported that after doctors, psychologists, chiropractors, acupuncturists, and the like had found nothing wrong with him, he visited a spiri-tual healer or, as the healer called herself, a practitioner of "white magic." This woman examined his tea leaves, looked at the patterns of rose petals floating in a bowl of water, felt his hands, read his palms, and told him that practitioners of black magic were sending him waves of extreme ill will. In short, she said, someone had put what amounted to a hex or a curse on him and he was feeling the physical effects of that curse.

Not to worry overmuch, she said, her magic, laden with appropriate amounts of herbal tea and some positive thoughts from him, would block the effects of the curse. She said that she would meditate, would imagine him standing within a bubble of white light, and would send positive thoughts of love in the direction of those who were wishing him ill will. She also taught him how to meditate and how to imagine himself in a bubble of white light. And she asked if he could figure out who might be attacking him.

My friend didn't know with any certainty, but he told her he believed that he'd pissed off certain people in our secret government by publishing books about them. He didn't know who they were, only that he was astounded that they could launch such an attack. Her advice was simple. Because he had been so worried about what they could do to him, he had made himself vulnerable to their ill will.

"Love conquers all," she said. And she explained that a "nonmagical" procedure for defeating curses against you, and, indeed, for defeating the effects of toxic people in general, is to wrap yourself in light and send the generator of ill will a warm ray of love. Seem illogical? My friend explained to me what she explained to him and I offer it to you as a kind of toxic cure-all.

No matter who and no matter what, when someone bears you ill will, malevolence strong enough to infect your mind—and we know how possible that is—you have got to have a kind of spiritual kung fu with which to defend yourself. Think about it: someone whose negative personality is so pervasive that he or she is able to put a curse on you just by being within the sphere of your life. Maybe it's your boss. Maybe it's someone you call a friend, but who is so negative you're afraid to confront him or her. Or maybe it's a parent or a relative. It can also be an enemy who actively and aggressively sends you negative energy, a curse if you want to call it that, just because that person wants to see you suffer. Of course, there are the more formal practitioners of evil, like my friend's college acquaintance, Doom. Let's include them all even though the most common negative energy you will encounter in your life is simply from a toxic individual.

What is your defense? I cite again the last line from one of my favorite poems, "Sir Gawain and the Green Knight," "Honi soit qui mal y pense." That was also the inscription worn by the Knights of the Garter in the court of Edward III. The phrase, more of an admonition than anything else, means that evil will come to him who thinks evil. So, if you can find a way not to think evil thoughts, conjure up evil ideations, you will have a defense against the coming of evil. How is this a defense against someone sending evil thoughts your way? It works because the sender of evil thoughts has projected himself into your mind. Your boss, for example, becomes a negative voice in your thoughts, challenging you, telling you you're not good enough, belittling you. So how do you keep him out of your thoughts? Send him love and good wishes. It's a way to keep him out of your mind. He pops up, give him love, he goes away.

If he pops up and you take the time and energy to send him hate, he wins because he's engaged you. Picture this. You're happy. You've seen a nice movie, had a nice evening, maybe met someone you like, and now the day's over and you're going off to bed. Oops, in pops Mr. Bad Boss. You interrupt your happy thoughts and engage this image. You counter ill will with your ill will. Mr. Bad Boss has effectively gotten in the way of your happiness and made you mad, made you hate, made you concentrate on evil. He wins. Just like a satanic person who succeeds not by being evil to you but by conning you into doing something evil to counter him, that's what Mr. Bad Boss has done. He has forced you to relinquish your happy self in order to deal with him. That's a victory.

Now turn this around. Mr. Bad Boss pops up and instead of sinking right into battle with him in your mind so as to compromise your own happiness, realize in that moment that it's all in your mind. You're the one puffing up Mr. Bad Boss into an oversize monster. Send him away with love all over him. Plaster him with love signs. Just the image of that may be so repugnant to you, you will send him away because you don't want that image in your mind. In this way, you've recognized that when evil pops in, you tend to enlarge it by acknowledging it and giving it an entrée, and then you make it worse by feeding it with your own hate. Swathe it with love first, bathe it and you with white light, and it will go away.

It is a kind of antimissile missile shield. Because, ultimately, love conquers all, when you send thoughts of love toward the source sending thoughts of evil in your direction, regardless of the intensity of malevolent thoughts coming your way, love will send them away while providing you with a mechanism that prevents you from feeding your enemy. It is, in its most basic terms, "Love thine enemy."

My friend took this spiritual healer's advice and bathed his enemies, wherever they came from, in a white light. And by refusing to get down into the ditch of hate with them, he defeated them. His symptoms disappeared, feelings of love washed away his sensations of anxiety, and he wound up healing himself. You can do exactly the same in your life by directing or focusing your consciousness on the light and on the love so as to prevent you from being taken over by agents of the darkness.

Rosemary Ellen Guiley

Dr. Rosemary Ellen Guiley is another person I like to listen to because of her story of angelic visions. These are not hallucinations, she says, not conjurations from the troubled minds of people who claim to see them. Angels are real, and her stories of people who see angels and why people see them bring hope to my Coast listeners as well as to me.

EXERCISES IN OUT OF BODY, PSYCHIC PROJECTION IN TIME, AND LEVITATION

H ey, George," the caller says. "Tell us how we can get out of our bodies the way you did back when you were a kid."

There are many techniques you can use to try to achieve an out-of-body experience, and meditation is one of the first steps you should take to prepare yourself. Even simple meditation is the gateway to an enhanced out-of-body experience in which your body functions slow down to a minimal level while your spirit travels over all of creation. For example, over the past few months in 2005, about 100,000 pilgrims have come to a forest in Bara, Nepal, to visit fifteen-year-old Ram Bahadur Bamjon who has been meditating nonstop for the past six months. People have called him the reincarnation of the Buddha and have marveled at his seemingly placid appearance, which has not changed.

No one sees him at night, when he is kept out of public view, so, as a Nepalese government investigator has said, no one knows what's really happening. Doctors who have looked at him, albeit from a distance, according to a New Zealand news website, reported that the child breathes normally, but he seems weak.

People making the pilgrimage to this forest in Nepal to see the child believe that he is the incarnation of the Buddha. His mother even has the same name as Buddha's mother. The child wears a shawl, according to the news website, across his shoulder and under his armpit the way Buddha did. So there is excitement over this child and what his ability to meditate all day long seems to portend.

My point here is not whether the child is the Buddha or not—although wouldn't it be very cool if he were?—but whether he is really in a meditative state or whether he has actually left his body. If this child is the physical repository of the Buddha, then might it not be possible that he has projected his psyche into another place or even another time while the body itself sits as if it's meditating?

I have hosted many a guest who has talked about the fine line between remote viewing and an actual out-of-body experience. In fact, according to my guest Paul Smith, author of *Reading the Enemy's Mind* and a frequent contributor to *UFO Magazine*, remote viewers were taught that not only were they not engaging in out-of-body experimentation but that in the line of work the coordinate remote viewers were doing, there was an actual danger in allowing oneself to become so involved with a target that the viewer almost left his body to go there. It was called "bi-location," a way of being in two places at the same time because your mind was there while your body stayed put.

Smith describes an incident in his book that took place during sessions in New York City when he had remote viewed a particularly beautiful landscape on a South Pacific atoll called Kwajalein. In fact, he perceived the area to be so beautiful and it left such a powerful impression in his mind that he kept traveling back to it, even as he walked along Broadway, a process called "reattachment." At one point, Paul became reattached to the target and the impression became so vivid that he felt he was actually there and caught himself as his body almost fell off the curb. This, he said, was a particularly graphic example of the dangers of approaching the line between remote viewing and leaving one's body.

What happens to the body, you can ask, if your consciousness decides to float somewhere else? You don't want to be standing at the intersection of Broadway and Seventh Avenue with taxis and busses bearing down on you or walking into an open manhole while your consciousness is somewhere on an atoll in the South Pacific.

The dangers of an uncontrolled astral projection or out-of-body experience notwithstanding, other guests have told our audience that there are many benefits to learning how to project your consciousness. For example, Dr. Alfred Taylor, a lecturer and researcher in the field, who has been a guest on *Coast*, has described the sense of empowerment that comes from practicing out-of-body travel. He has repeatedly explained that the premise of out of body is not the sense of detachment from yourself, but the grand sense of attachment with the totality of the universe. It is an experience that can be so sublime in its embrace of the great link that unites all creation that novices sometimes forget that they have bodies they must return to. Therefore, Dr. Taylor suggests that people who want to learn these techniques must first ground themselves in meditative practices. I heartily agree with this because I know from my own out-of-body experience that I was so shocked at the realization that I was floating above myself that I returned to my body almost at once and have longed for that experience again for the ensuing forty years. But, my guest experts on *Coast* have told me, if you practice meditation, you can build in an auto-response mechanism to stress, such as the shock caused by recognizing that you've left your own body.

Someone I know in the UFO community also reported a

strange out-of-body experience during remote-viewing training a few years ago. She said that she had been working with
one of the remote-viewing trainers and during one of the sessions, she experienced an odd vibration sensation, almost as if
she were picking up waves from somewhere. She felt she was
moving, but she knew that she was seated. So she opened her
eyes and noticed that she was indeed moving and that she
could see her own body in front of her. She said that the recognition of what she was looking at was so shocking that she immediately slammed right back into her body, and the session
was over. This reminds me of exactly what happened to me
when I had my out-of-body experience as a child. This young
woman, too, reported that she wanted to experience that event
again because it imparted to her a sense that there was much,
much more to the universe and creation than she had experienced previously.

William Buhlman, an out-of-body and astral projection
researcher to whom Dr. Taylor has linked his own website, has
written that there are many benefits to an out-of-body experience, not the least of which is the knowledge that the experiencer is part of a great link uniting the entire universe. The
release from the bounds of one's own body brings a person a
sense of euphoria because the human form is no longer a limitation to one's consciousness. That's why it's so important to
reduce one's self-awareness as a prerequisite to any out-of-
body experience or other psychic experience. Self-awareness is
a reminder of the physical limitation of the body. When she is
not self-aware, her mind is free to transcend the body and experience the limitlessness of being part of the greater universe.

Buhlman also suggests that people who have experienced
an out-of-body event become convinced that there is a part of

us that exists separate and independent from our physical bodies. I can personally attest to the truth of that. When I looked down at my own body from the ceiling and realized that I was not dreaming, I knew, in that very instant, that there is a part of us that is not tied to the physical nature of our bodies. Call it the soul, call it the spirit, call it whatever you want to. Whatever you call it, if you experience the mind-boggling perception of looking at yourself you will know that there is something about human existence that is immortal. Once you know that, as people who have had near death experiences have reported, you know that, in the words of my friend and repeat guest Joel Martin, "We don't die."

Many people have reported that while on life support during cardiac surgery, they were able to look down on the events taking place on the operating table. I have to say that if what these people have said is true, then they have indeed become endowed with a unique vision, a vision that human beings have a connection to the universe not limited by the confines of their own bodies. People who have had these experiences also have a different take on the nature of humanity because they enjoy an enhanced ability to perceive what it is to be human and what it is to transcend our three-dimensional form. I would love to interview some of these people about their experiences and to ask them how what they saw changed their perspectives on life. I would also like to know whether having had a near death out-of-body experience made them less afraid of dying, now that they know there is an immortality to the human spirit.

Dr. Shafica Karagulla also had much to say about the nature of an out-of-body experience on the basis of her interviews with people who tested at the upper end of the scale for higher-sensory perception. She wrote that people who were able to perceive auras—shades of light—around other people, or perceive the directions or inclinations of others, had sometimes told her that they had weird sensations that they could leave their own bodies. These stories fascinated my aunt because, as dedicated to paranormal research as she was, she was a scientist by training, a medical investigator, and ultimately wanted to be able to duplicate and measure the kinds of phenomena she encountered. Therefore, in testing her subjects to see if they could pick up psychic signals about what image on a card she was concealing from them or measuring their EEG patterns, Dr. Karagulla would ask about such things as visions; auditory, olfactory, or visual hallucinations that seemed real; and, ultimately, sensations that the subjects were leaving their bodies.

Many of Shafica's subjects told her that they had never spoken of their higher-sensory perceptions until they became part of Shafica's research group. Of course, they had mentioned their belief about their HSP to friends, and that ultimately led them to Shafica, but they had never talked openly about it or confided to others that they could pick up signals that might be interpreted as reading someone else's mind. Yet, and this is one of the things that out-of-body experiencers share, even though many subjects desired to keep their secrets close, they reported that they were desperate to learn about their abilities. I can reveal that I am the very same way. The simple fact that I once had an out-of-body experience gave me a burning desire to find out as much about my own spirituality as possible. Like many of Shafica's subjects, my out-of-body experience drove me to learn more about it, to ascertain its nature, and to see what I could find out about the eternal nature of the human spirit.

Some of my aunt's subjects suggested to her that they could perceive maladies in others. I think what they meant was that through an out-of-body experience they were able to see malformations in a person's aura that indicated either an illness or an injury. This aspect of out-of-body experiences fascinated Shafica because she related it directly to an ability that Edgar Cayce demonstrated to his followers. Cayce, reportedly, was not only a prophet, but he was a healer, able to diagnose all kinds of maladies and communicate with the stricken part of a patient's body so as to effect a healing. Today, many Cayce scholars will tell you that doctors were confounded by Cayce's abilities to heal the sick. Joel Martin, in *The Haunting of the Presidents,* writes that Cayce tended to President Woodrow Wilson during the latter part of his presidency after Wilson's stroke left him incapacitated. Because Wilson's wife was so afraid of the negative publicity regarding a prophet visiting the White House, she had Cayce secreted in through side doors so that he wouldn't be recognized.

These stories of out-of-body experiencers being able to either diagnose or heal others or effect what Buhlman calls a "spontaneous healing" are part of the benefits that he talks about when he writes that an out-of-body experience is not something to be feared, it's something that will transform one's life. I know this to be the case from my own experience and Shafica Karagulla, who studied this phenomena, also realized this benefit.

In many ways, a deliberate out-of-body experience that involves projecting one's psyche so that it seems to float outside the limitations of one's body is much like lucid dreaming. In fact, following the lucid dreaming steps we talked about earlier and practicing the steps of focus and visualizing an object, such as your bedside clock, as you fall asleep so that when you look at the clock again and can't read the numbers you realize you're dreaming, is precisely what you will do in one form of out-of-body projection. Lucid dreaming is actually an early step to out-of-body projection because the realization that you're dreaming and that you're possessed with all the powers of a dreamer is the mechanism that allows you to find a target and project yourself there. Physical sleep is the transition phase that turns off self-awareness. That's why many people say that an out-of-body experience is simply a more advanced and intentional extension of lucid dreaming.

The most basic preparation for an out-of-body experience is to surround yourself with a white light during your mantra and meditation sessions. Here's what you do. As you picture your negative thoughts or daily concerns floating away on a stream, imagine that the sun is shining very brightly. It's so bright that you are surrounded by the light, a completely white light that blots out everything else. You will take that light with you as if you're in a bubble. This bubble of light will protect you against evil and against navigating yourself into bad places. Remember, when you begin the following exercises to astral project yourself out there into the multidimensional universe, wear your bubble of light because no matter where you go, it will protect you and keep you whole.

The next basic preparation for an out-of-body experience is a mental version of one of the lucid dreaming exercises. Instead of focusing only on a physical object in the real world, such as the bedside clock or your hand or wristwatch as you fall asleep, to prepare for an out-of-body experience, you can also focus on an image in your mind. Do this at bedtime. Begin with your normal mantra repetition to put you into a meditative state, discarding all thoughts of the day and laying aside your awareness of your own body and concerns that may be driving you. Now, after you've made your connection and feel yourself getting tired, practice putting an image into your mind of something familiar, whose every outline and shape you can trace with your mind. Maybe it's an image of your loved one or your child. Maybe it's an image of a parent.

The experts say that you should focus on this image as you fall asleep, practicing it every night just after completing your mantra. Eventually, you will discover that, just like a lucid dream, you will fall asleep, but will see the image and it will remind you that you are conscious of what you are doing even though you are asleep. At that point, if you look back at yourself, you will notice that you can see your own body on the bed. This is precisely what happened to me when I had my out-of-body experience. Once you notice your own body, assume that what you are looking at is true and then try to navigate to a known location, something close by. Think about floating down the hallway of your house or apartment to another room to see what's going on. Maybe float over to a window and peer out.

Start out very slowly, but be bold. If you practice this rigorously, what you will find is that you will be able to visit friends, coworkers, your boss, anyone. Simply by picturing their faces in your out-of-body state, visualizing that you are in front of them or listening to them, and visualizing a setting where you and your target might encounter one another will take you there. There is no time continuum, no space continuum. It is as if you are the character Q on *Star Trek: The Next Generation.* Think of it and it becomes true. Will it and it's a done deal. You can travel to any place, project yourself to any location and to any time. Think of it just like you have all the power of a dream state. But in this state you know you're dreaming so that all the things you can do in a dream, you can do in an astral projected state.

The other technique you can use is to focus on a specific thing. When we talked about lucid dreaming, we talked about your bedside clock or something on the table. This time, because you are going to project yourself to a different spot, try to focus on an inage of an object at another location. William Buhlman suggests that you focus on something inside your own house or apartment. Guests on *Coast* have suggested that you focus on something in an entirely different physical location. I think you can start simply by visualizing something in the next room. Maybe, as Buhlman suggests, a favorite couch or a chair. Stare at the object before you go to bed. Familiarize yourself with some of the intricate details of the object. I remember that I used to focus on a leather couch we once had in our living room when I was a kid. I knew every crack in that leather, every place that one of the little copper or brass buttons that held the leather pieces was turning green or had become tarnished. I know that today I can go back to that very couch in an astral projection exercise and maybe even see my father sitting in it.

Just as you do in the facial imaging exercise, this time focus on the object as you fall asleep. Do your mantra, meditate, and then, begin the very deliberate process of holding the image of the object in your mind and letting your mind's eye run over every part of the object. Bring the object up in great detail so that all your attention is focused on the seams, the cracks, the variations in color, and the way the outlines of the shape differ from one part to the other. It's easier if in your mind there is a psychological or emotional connection to the object you're visualizing.

Just as in lucid dreaming and in meditating on your mantra, the out-of-body exercises require practice and repetition. You should try to have some fun with them every night by focusing on the same object and seeing if it turns up in your dreams. Actually, you're conditioning your mind to hold the image even after you are asleep and then recognizing the image once you think you're dreaming. What out-of-body researchers and experiencers will tell you is that you're not actually dreaming, you've projected your spirit. Assuming, therefore, that you hold the image of a favorite object in a different spot even after your body has gone to sleep, you have successfully projected yourself to that object in that spot. Now you have to recognize that you've projected yourself to that spot, and therein lies the science of astral projection.

You can also train yourself in the art of out-of-body projection by using different sound frequencies that affect the different hemispheres of your brain. This technique, pioneered and trademarked by Robert Monroe, founder of the Monroe Institute, is known as the Hemi-Synch®. Monroe is one of my private favorite pioneers in out-of-body experiences not just because his techniques have drawn so much recognition but because his background was in radio, broadcasting, and writing. I continue to be fascinated by the career of this individual, who began as a director and copywriter for radio stations in Ohio, became a producer in his own right and then a network owner, created many radio game shows for the industry in the

1950s, and was even a music composer, expanding his career into the movie industry. By the 1970s, Bob Monroe had become one of the earlier developers of programming for the fledgling cable television industry.

Monroe was still an engineer at heart and, maybe because of his radio background, was fascinated by the effects of different sound frequencies, particularly as they influenced human awareness during deep sleep. In fact, he was an early innovator of "learn while you sleep" technology, believing that the human mind simply didn't shut down in sleep. These experiments with deep-sleep learning further encouraged him to undertake research in the nature of consciousness. Would, he asked, a varying sound frequency not only promote the receptivity of the mind to learn facts and concepts but actually allow the mind to leave the body? It was a tantalizing concept. What if the supernatural abilities that one experiences in a dream state could be turned into a reality simply by finding the right frequencies piped directly into the appropriate location on each brain hemisphere so as to synchronize the brain waves between the hemispheres?

The human brain is actually composed of two separate but connected hemispheres. Each hemisphere, although there is redundancy and parallelism, is essentially dedicated to functions and often works on different mental processes at the same time. This means that the human brain, unlike the brains of the our hominid ancestors, is asymmetrical. As a result, doctors can measure the different electronic patterns of each hemisphere separately. The two hemispheres are connected by a thick bundle of neurons called the corpus callosum, which acts as the essential communications mechanism between the right and left sides of your brain. For Robert Monroe, bringing the two hemispheres into a kind of synchronization was one of the ways, along with verbal suggestions, that he could stimulate an out-of-body experience.

Because, according to his official biography on the Monroe Institute website, Bob Monroe did not believe in sending people off to do work he should be doing himself, he became his own test subject. In 1958, he began to perfect a state, which he described as a consciousness separate and apart from his own body. He coined the phrase "out-of-body experience," and it became the generic name for a state in which the experiencer's awareness actually leaves his or her body and is able to travel to other places and even other times. He detailed some of his work in his 1971 book, *Journeys Out of the Body,* a revolutionary work that gave a scientific methodology to a practice that medicine men, prophets, shamans, witches, and seers had been following for thousands of years. Suddenly, the stories of what Edgar Cayce and others were able to accomplish made sense in the real world because Monroe was able to explain a state of consciousness, which up to then had been only explainable as wizardry, something to be feared.

By 1974, Monroe had turned his discoveries into an actual item, described as an "audio-guidance technology" called Hemi-Sync®, short for hemispheric synchronization. This became the entrée for students, researchers, psychologists, and just about anyone interested in exploring the nature of consciousness, to facilitate an out-of-body state simply by listening and being guided to an altered level of consciousness. And in 1994, just a year before his death, Monroe published his final book, *Ultimate Journey,* about the relationship of the physical world to the limits of human potential. If you want to pursue the formal Monroe Institute training protocols, you can easily find them on the web by clicking on monroeinstitute.org or by looking up Robert Monroe on the Internet.

The ironic thing about Robert Monroe and his out-of-body experiences was that at first he didn't realize what they were when they were happening. In fact, it took him years to understand the nature of this phenomenon. He had begun by experimenting with sounds of different frequencies, especially as ways to calm himself when he was about to go to sleep, when at times not connected to his audio experiments, his body began to be seized by vibrations. He thought he was experiencing tremors, but he wasn't sick. When at one point he noticed that after sensing the, by now, familiar vibrations, he could see his own body from above, he thought he was losing his mind. Of course, doctors couldn't really help him because in the early 1960s no one outside of Eastern philosophers or practitioners of Eastern religions knew what an out-of-body event was. It was Bob Monroe's readings in parapsychology that led him to an understanding of the experiences he was having. At that point, he began to experiment with what he was perceiving, stretching the bounds of each event, and traveling through space and time. For a more detailed description of how Robert Monroe discovered the nature of out-of-body experiences, read D. Scott Rogo's *Leaving the Body,* which also details the many different techniques you can use to train yourself in astral projection.

Scott Rogo explains the Monroe technique as a complex series of mental imagery exercises in which a person can induce a vibrational state, the indicator that the person is ready to separate from his or her body and go traveling. Rogo writes that Monroe practiced placing himself in a state between waking and sleeping, focusing on specific objects, and thinking about projecting himself toward a certain spot ahead of him. His technique involved imaging a point six feet from his forehead and about thirty degrees above the center of his forehead. Monroe went so far, Rogo explains, as to measure this thirty-degree angle with a protractor so that he would be accurate.

Gradually relaxing each and every muscle progressively while visualizing a specific image and then projecting his thoughts at a point six feet ahead and thirty degrees above him, Monroe exercised control of his consciousness. Then, he imagined, but did not budge physically, rotating his body at ninety degrees to its position. You can practice this, too. Imagine that you are lying, hands at your sides, eyes closed, focusing on a point about six feet ahead of you and then imagining that you can rotate your body 90 degrees. Try this as an exercise to see if you can visualize this. This is how Monroe trained himself. And this is what he did to generate a series of vibrations that were the precursor of physical manifestations to Monroe's separation from his body.

There are sleep specialists who say that the vibrations Monroe and other out-of-body practitioners experience are natural occurrences that take place during a presleep phase called a hypnogogic state. This state is also accompanied by something called "sleep paralysis," where your muscles tighten and you feel you can't move at all. Oddly enough, the same sleep specialists say that those who claim to have been abducted by extraterrestrials and are paralyzed before being transported to a space ship are actually only experiencing a hypnogogic state with dreams that seem like reality. You can be the judge of that. Many of the same doctors say that what Monroe actually experienced was akin to this hypnogogic state and that the vibrations he wrote about were simply the result of his muscles going into spasm, what is known as a clonic tightening, at the onset of sleep. Again, it's a matter of what a person wants to believe. Me, I believe what Monroe wrote.

Another *Coast* guest, Dr. Bruce Goldberg, author of *Astral Voyages,* also describes the physical phenomena associated with the entrance into an out-of-body state. His description of a "sinking and floating" sensation also corresponds with my own out-of-body experience when I was eleven. His description of "a paralyzed body" and various impressions of "roaring or gushing" sounds certainly corresponds to what many psychologists and sleep experts have referred to as indicators of a hypnogogic state, the transition of your physical body into a sleep state while you are still conscious of what is happening. However, the perception of seeing your own body from a different perspective, either looking down at it from above or seeing it in front of you, realizing what you're seeing—in Bruce's words, "blacking out and awaking back in your physical body"—are impressions associated with an initial out-of-body experience. These describe my impressions almost exactly.

Dr. Goldberg also describes an event in which an experiencer, not exactly sure of whether she is asleep or awake, keeps seeing herself in her own bedroom, even while knowing that she is asleep. A friend of mine experienced this on a number of occasions but wrote it off as either a dream that he was having or to waking up momentarily, looking around, and then falling back to sleep. At a certain point, however, my friend said that he "knew" he was asleep and that he was dreaming he was in his bedroom. Nothing strange about that. But it was the sensation he was having during that dream that unnerved him because he felt that the dream had him trapped even though he knew he was dreaming. So what's that all about? You know you're dreaming, you know where you are, but realize that you have to exert a conscious effort to change the scene in order to get out of a dream. That's what my friend described; he told me how even though the scene would change, he would always find himself back inside his bedroom again in between scene changes. That, in Dr. Goldberg's astral paradigm, would be an initial out-of-body experience. It is a phenomenon that you might encounter as you begin to exercise your out-of-body muscles.

Even if you are only aware of the presence of your physical body next to you or below you, you have achieved the first stage of astral projection, according to Bruce Goldberg. In fact, Dr. Goldberg, who suggests that not only can human beings get in touch with their past lives, they can also understand and inhabit their future lives, has laid out a five-stage scheme for astral projection. Stage One, as Bruce describes it, is the initial separation of astral body and physical body. In Stage Two, you are floating a few feet away from your own physical body. This may be akin to a sense of floating above your body while you are being treated at an accident scene or during an operation. In Stage Three, you may be hundreds of feet away but still in familiar surroundings. For example, you may be roaming around your house at night while your physical body is in bed. You don't see your body, but you are familiar with the setting so there's no sense of anxiety about where you are. The more you practice out-of-body projection, however, the more comfortable you will probably become with the separated state and feel it is okay to wander a greater distance from your body.

In Stage Four the out-of-body traveler is not bound by the need to stay close to his or her physical body or remain in familiar settings. On a basic level, Stage Four might be a real goal because if you have the ability to project yourself thousands of miles away or years away, you have the ability to empower yourself by seeing the future. How do you do this? Bruce Goldberg suggests that this is actually only a matter of will. If you want to project yourself someplace or somewhere, since thought travels at the speed of light—Colonel Philip Corso once said that thought is faster than the speed of light—you need only think it and you will be there. Imagine that you are aware that you have separated from your body. You are in familiar surroundings. It would be a dream except for the fact that you have an awareness that your body is in the next room. You think of a friend, your boss, your office, your child, and you are there. You have questions and your questions are answered. You think of yourself at old age and you see yourself at old age. It is your thought that propels you through space and across time. This is what Bruce Goldberg suggests is the travel methodology for an experienced out-of-body practitioner.

Bruce Goldberg describes Stage Five as the plateau of pure spiritual enlightenment. It is here, he says, that you encounter your spiritual guide or even a guardian angel. I read about this phenomenon when I first read the Carlos Castaneda accounts of Yaqui Indian shaman Don Juan. In Don Juan's conversations, he described an out-of-body state in which he encountered his guides and allies, spirits who helped him understand the real nature of the universe. I have also read accounts by parapsychologists of counseling sessions in which they guide a client into a meeting with the client's own private guru, who is always present but whose advice is jammed by what Paul Smith, Ingo Swann, and Hal Puthoff might describe as analytical overlay. This guru, the parapsychologist counselor wrote, was contacted by the client's traveling down many stairs in his mind during a visualization session until he reached a cave with a lake. There, floating on the lake, was the guru who showed the traveler how to project himself into the future, into the past, and inhabit realms on other planes of the multiverse. Bruce Goldberg suggests that at Stage Five of astral projection, one can achieve this level of enlightenment so as to understand that the true nature of creation is not bounded by time or space or our three-dimensional reality, but is actually infinite.

All of these stages start with self-preparation and a desire to achieve an out-of-body state. And no matter which procedure you follow at first, if you have bathed yourself in white light and have asked for protection from evil during your mantra state, you can achieve the initial stages of an out-of-body experience. If you practice a visualization, projection, or rotation regimen consistently for a few weeks either at bedtime or just on awakening from sleeping, you may begin to experience the same physical vibrations Monroe did, which Bruce Goldberg also describes. Don't be afraid. These are not harmful even though they may seem odd or uncomfortable at first. Learn to bring these vibrations on almost at will by conditioning yourself to go into this state quickly. At that point, you are ready for the next stage.

Scott Rogo writes that Monroe explained that he didn't just practice jumping out of his body all at once. He did it by stages, experimenting tentatively with extensions of his consciousness until he felt he was ready to leave the physical nest. Monroe did this by imagining that he could extend his psychic hand beyond his physical hand. Picture this yourself. Close your eyes and imagine that you can see your hand extending beyond your hand. Put your hand near an object and visualize that your fingers and then your entire hand are grasping that object. How does it feel? Can you sense any vibrations emanating from that object?

Now, go through the Monroe regimen on your own for a week, maybe two, and see if after you have imagined you can rotate your body at a ninety-degree angle from the point ahead of you and sense the resulting vibrations, that you can extend just your hand beyond itself. Practice this as well. First grasp an object. Then, do something really bold. As you visualize your hand extending, extend it right through a wall or a solid object. Feel the vibrations? Allow yourself to sense the different vibrations of different types of surfaces. This is what Monroe did as he sought to assume control of his out-of-body experience.

Now you're ready. Following the Monroe procedure, you will see that once he successfully managed to extend his psychic hand through his physical hand, he realized that he was capable of separating from his body. The next step was to separate himself entirely. He did this, when he was experiencing the vibrations, by telling himself that he was rising out of his body. He thought it and he did it. Monroe was able to look down and see his body on the bed. He was fully aware of what was happening and that he had levitated himself right out from his own physical body. Now he was ready to travel.

He began by going into the next room, visualizing objects in the room, and traveling to see his children in their rooms. Then he was ready for more extensive journeys out of his body, experiences he writes about in *Far Journeys* and *Ultimate Journey*, through space and through time itself.

What about you? If you follow this technique and series of procedures so as to make them routine, you can achieve many of the same results that Monroe and others achieved. Practice and you will soon find that you can actually see yourself levitating out of your body. Next, you will encounter the barriers of solid objects. You can choose to travel around them, going through open doors and windows. Or you can choose to travel through the solid objects themselves. You will have to attune yourself to the different vibrations you will feel as you move through walls, doors, glass, and, even through other people. I can't tell you what you will feel because different experiencers have said that these are unique sensations. All I can say is that many people who practice astral projection say that they are aware, when they move through solid objects, that the objects seem as though they are actually alive. I know that may sound strange, but if the entire planet is alive, then maybe life is actually a kind of frequency and, like light across a spectrum, some frequencies seem to us as not alive when they really are. But, many people who have projected their psyches caution that if you move through a solid object, you will experience the odd sensation that you have passed through a living entity.

Once you've recognized that you have successfully projected yourself, what are you going to do next? I suggest you keep it close to home in the very beginning. But as you expand your abilities, try to visit relevant targets. For example, because in an out-of-body state, you wield powers that are not bound by the limitations of your body, you can see things that you can't do in a normal waking state. Travel to your office. You will find that you can actually sit with your coworkers, your boss, your clients. In a benevolent way, you can hone in on their own lives, thoughts, desires. You will find that you will gain a deeper understanding of who they are and what they want. This is the beauty of astral projection. You can learn about the humanity of other people once you are in an out-of-body state.

Can you imagine how much more effective you will be as a person, as a family member, as a friend, or as a coworker? Think about your ability to travel into the future whenever you are faced with a difficult situation at work or in life. If you have mastered even some of the techniques of astral projection, you will have given yourself the ability to deal with other people, particularly in difficult situations, in ways that allow you to embrace their needs because your vision will be all-encompassing. You will have a serenity about yourself. You will be unflappable because you will sense what people want and expect from you no matter how they try to deflect it. Picture yourself at work, secure in the knowledge that you have an extra sense about what's happening around you. Nothing will ever be threatening to you again. And above all, because you have established a link with the entire universe, with all creation, you will reach a level of understanding that allows you to love everything that has been, is, or ever will be created. This is a majestic state because you will see, over your many forays out of body, that the one force in the universe that unites all and survives all is love. And that makes you a powerful individual because you know the power of love.

My Storytellers

Then there is Lionel Fanthorpe, one of my favorite story-teller guests. He says he has found a miniature mummy in an exhibit in White City, New Mexico, not far from Roswell. The mummy, according to his description and the photograph on our Coast to Coast *website looks almost exactly like the aliens that Roswell historians have described. Could one of the bodies of the ET pilots have wound up in this museum? Then Fanthorpe tells the story of the haunted bookstore in San Antonio, Texas, built over the ruins of the very spot where some of the bodies of the brave Texans who defended the Alamo against General Santa Ana were buried. At this bookshop, mysteriously every night, no matter how carefully books are shelved at the end of every day, the same pile of books are found on the floor in the morning when the owner comes to open up the store.*

Another favorite guest that I can listen to for hours is Dr. Paul Pearsall, formerly of Detroit but now in Hawaii. Dr. Pearsall has lectured on business, education, psychology, and humor. A clinical neuropsychologist, Paul is anything but straitlaced. He comes on the show and tells our listening audience to do crazy things, break out of their ruts, laugh themselves out of colds and flu into health, and not to worry about growing old. He is one of my favorite guests because you don't have to do anything but listen. Just listening will get you through whatever life crisis you're confronting.

INTUITION, INDIGO CHILDREN, CRYSTAL CHILDREN, AND *CHILDHOOD'S END*

I t's almost two in the morning now. And it's Christmas. I spent the evening before the show, which I devoted to open lines so everyone who wanted someone to talk to tonight would be able to find me on the other end of the phone, going out into the world of Los Angeles on Christmas Eve. I remember that when I was growing up in Detroit when the night wind would come in off the Great Lakes sometimes bringing lake snow, I would feel as if the world was touched by magic. So now in Los Angeles, I go out into the early night, maybe stopping to see the last-minute shoppers at the Galleria or at the Beverly Connection and all the while thinking about those Christmas Eves when I was a kid. Maybe, I thought back then, just maybe if I strained my eyes to see into the darkness over the lake, I would catch a glimpse of a sleigh or reindeer against a third-quarter moon. And sometimes I even thought I did.

"Tell me about how intuition has helped you, George?" The caller is from Maine, way east of the Rockies. She's been up through the whole show and will try to catch a couple of hours of sleep before the kids come roaring downstairs to rifle through the boxes under the tree. She'll have to be up when she hears the first stirrings, though, because she will shake out the ashes from the woodstove, flip open the chimney flue damper, close the check damper, and open the bottom damper to let the fire grow. She will throw a couple logs on top and the house will warm in just a few minutes so that the children, excited by the brightly colored boxes with their names on them, won't be chilled as they set out their presents. Maybe she'll put a cast iron pot of water on top of the stove and throw some cinnamon sticks, orange peels, and cloves in it to give a Christmas bouquet to the morning. I'm listening to her and thinking of my own kids on Christmas mornings too long ago when I couldn't imagine myself at this age.

"You got any more stories about intuition?" she asks.

As a matter of fact, I do. Lots, I tell her. You see, most of my guests who are specialists in intuitive thinking have a great deal to say about their friends and sometime clients who have sought their advice. In fact some of the stories I hear from guests on *Coast* are so bizarre, I wonder whether I'm hearing about intuition, remote viewing, out of body, or actual time travel. Then I certainly have my own story about how intuition saved me from a serious injury, a story that won't go away and that I keep telling anyone who has any doubts about the power of intuition and the necessity of listening to it, even if it defies logic. Here's the story.

My intuition once kept me out of a car accident. I'm from Detroit, so I love cars. I love driving, even on L.A. freeways, where driving can be an endurance test. But a while back I was driving in St. Louis when I came upon a familiar intersection. You know how most people gauge the traffic at familiar intersections, especially when we know how long it takes a light to change and how close we can coast before we have to apply the brakes. Same with me. I pulled up to the light, let the car slow down, waited for the yellow light to come on for the crossing traffic, and timed it so that when my light turned green I would be cruising through the intersection. Only as I approached the light, knowing it would turn green in a matter of seconds, I had a feeling of negativity and strangeness, a feeling of impending doom. This feeling was so overpowering that as the light changed to green, instead of hitting the gas, I hit the brake. Cars behind me honked in fury as I slowed down, but I was listening to another signal. Then, as I stopped in front of a green light, waiting for I knew not what, barreling down the cross street came another car, bigger than mine, that would have taken me out had I proceeded into the intersection. This was a classic example of how intuition, or maybe a guardian angel talking to my intuition, clearly saved me from serious injury. I listened to my intuition even though all logic told me that nothing was wrong.

Friends tried to dissuade me from believing my intuition had saved me. They said that my peripheral vision had picked up the car coming down the street and I simply reacted to it like any well-trained driver who doesn't even realize he is reacting to stimuli. Other people said that I actually heard the noise of an approaching car and reacted to that even if I couldn't see it. No intuition there, they said, you simply heard it. However, my windows were rolled up and the radio was playing. I couldn't hear any outside noises whatsoever, so that theory is a nonstarter. Nope. For me, I know in my heart that my intuitive sense of danger picked up the threat and I listened to it instead of relying on my other senses.

Life is just like coming to a four-way intersection, especially modern life with conflicts among family, work, friends, and relationships. They all seem to come to the same intersection at the same time. You can imagine exactly how every single rule in your life can conflict with others. It's just as if you've come to a four-way intersection with no Stop signs or traffic lights. What do you do? First, keep your eyes open, and I mean your intuitive eyes as well as your physical eyes. It's been my experience that most people come to these intersections with eyes blindfolded, windshield obstructed, ears plugged up with earphone music, and a head cold slowing down all their thought processes. Most people simply don't have enough information to make a decision, let alone the confidence to listen to their own intuition telling them what's going on right before their eyes. If you are willing to listen to yourself, unplug your ears, take your blinders off, let in fresh air, and use your senses to make the right decision. You will be able to tell if the intersection is clear before you go.

Folks who practice out-of-body projections or who exercise their intuition on a regular basis know a big secret about creation, a secret that all of us believe but few act on. We know that there's something after this life, although we call it by different names. Regardless of how you define the afterlife, you're going to pass out of this plane, cross over, and you will encounter life as a spirit. What I hope you have picked up thus far are the rules of living and dealing with others and the overwhelming experience of love that you encountered during your astral projection events, and that they have shown you that if you have followed the golden rule of relationships, your spirit, passing out of this plane, will not be obstructed.

The golden rule, as humanity evolves to a new era of embracing its ability to travel in time and different dimensions, is to spread love to other beings out of your being and to be curious like a child about everything in the world. As people who have undergone near death experiences have told us, we're here to learn and here to love. Everything we've talked about concerning our innate ability to navigate through the multiverse reinforces the basic rule that love is the golden thread that unites all of us, enables us to live longer, live healthier, live within a protective spiritual envelope, and enables us to reach out to our fellow human beings, even the ones who say they wish us ill. If, as you venture out along the psychic superhighway, you have any questions about what to do and how to do it, send out a beam of love first because love conquers all and love will show the way. It's all you need at the initial levels of psychic travel.

Listening to your intuitive voice can help you live longer, happier, and more productively. For example, one of my *Coast* guests is Dr. Steven R. Hawks, whose National Institute of Intuitive Eating promotes a diet that's a nondiet, but which is based almost entirely on intuition. I like his program because it's a clear example of how listening to your intuition defeats everything people say about food: what to eat, when to eat, and how to eat. Dr. Hawks made the news after reports of his diet turned up on CNN and other Internet news sites under headlines about how one man says that eating ice cream can help you lose weight. It was kind of a man bites dog story.

If you look at what Dr. Hawks is saying—and sure, you can eat that bowl of chili if that's what your body is calling for—it makes sense. Hawks says that your body expresses its own needs for nutrition, which you pick up as an intuition driving your interest in foods. Most of us don't eat intuitively. We eat what we're told, forced to clean our plates as kids when we're just not hungry, forced by our schedules to jam in food when we're thinking about something else so we overeat just to compensate, and relegated to eating in front of a television, a device designed to sap our energy, intuition, confidence, and replace it with anger, frustration, anxiety, and—yes—hatred. Don't get me started on this. I fully believe that if extraterrestrials wanted to take over Earth, reduce this planet's population to a demoralized pack of self-hating rodents killing each other over a piece of rotting flesh, they would have invented television and brought it here. So don't eat in front of a television set whatever you do. It's an automatic weight-gaining mechanism, designed to be that way by the very same folks who bring you the commercials for diets to lose the TV weight you've gained.

Dr. Hawks looks at all the ways we eat, when and how we eat, and says that our eating habits remove us from the act of feeding our bodies. We're too busy stressing out about other things to let our bodies absorb the nutritional aspect of eating. For example, we eat too fast. We eat so fast, he says, that our bodies don't even realize we're full. We just look at the supersize meals because we like big burgers, big fries, and big SUVs. By the time we've paid for this, we have to eat it so we don't throw money away. Hence, we eat more than we need and gain weight.

Dr. Hawks says that the very nature of fast food can be a danger because fast food means fast eating. Fast eating means that the body can't regulate its intake. So we eat more than we need and gain weight. Regardless of what we're eating, eating too quickly and without thinking trips up the body's intake gauge. It's that gauge that often tells us what we need, what we have cravings for, and what will satisfy us. By defeating that gauge, we are using the wrong kind of input to defeat our intuitive sense of what we should be eating and when we're full.

What does intuitive eating tell us? It says that each person, especially if that person is not trying to look like someone he or she is not, has a natural intuitive ability to sense when hunger strikes and what foods will satisfy that hunger. Of course, eating more calories than you burn will mean putting on weight. And of course, some foods are higher in calories than others. And of course, we all know about the dangers of high-fat, high-sugar, high-carbohydrate foods and foods of empty nutritional value. That being said, we also know that many diets actually cause weight gain because diets can be artificial. You restrict certain foods until you reach a certain weight. Then, happy you've achieved a weight goal, you go back to those foods again and gain weight.

Most diets are anti-intuitive. Back in the 1970s, I remember the first all-protein diets. The more meat you eat, the more the body has to work to burn it. Thus, the more you eat the more weight you lose. Great idea, except that for most of us it didn't work. Worse, you had to drink gallons of water a day as part of the diet. The water was the best part of a diet because filling up with water makes your stomach feel full and you eat less.

In the 1980s we were all worried about food combinations. Don't have cheese on your burger. Don't have potatoes with your pot roast. I could go on, but you get the idea. There was science behind this program, but it was a science alien to most of us because it ran counter to what we wanted. Our intuition was telling us that we wanted certain foods and that if we ate them we would feel satisfied. Then we wouldn't overeat. Guess what, that intuition is correct.

Dr. Hawks promotes a program that says, first, listen to what your body is telling you. Ask what foods you have a hankering for. Eat the foods so as to enjoy them, not to cram them in. Try to eat at times when you can contemplate what you're eating. If you're balancing your breakfast burrito with your coffee while you're merging onto the Hollywood Freeway from the 405 or trying to get off the Jersey Turnpike at exit 14 at eight-thirty in the morning, you're probably not listening to what your body says you should be eating. You're probably lucky enough just to keep the coffee from spilling over the cup holder onto your pants. The demands of the real world are get-ting between you and your intuitive signal.

The answer, Dr. Hawks says, is to figure out when you can eat, even on a busy schedule, and eat the foods you want rather than the foods you think you should have. Eating what you want, even if it's categorized as unhealthy, will satisfy what your body is asking for and cut down on overeating. As for eat-ing on the run, Dr. Hawks suggests that if you like certain foods, stock up on them and bring them along as snacks. That will cut down on overeating, too. The trick is that you can eat food in any combinations, in any amounts—as long as you don't stuff yourself—and at any time during the day. Does this nondiet diet work?

Dr. Hawks reports research that says people who eat what they want when they want to have fewer weight problems and succumb less to binge eating and fad foods. Therefore, in this way, your intuition, when you listen to that signal, can help you live healthier, live longer, and lose weight.

"But, George," another caller asks. "How many people ac-tually believe in this stuff? I believe it. But do most people re-ally believe in the supernatural, in God? They sure don't act like they do."

In fact, I tell my caller, according to a 2005 survey, over 95 percent of Americans said they believed in God. At times, it does seem as if there is a disconnect for some people, like the ones fighting with each other on toy store lines on the opening day of Christmas shopping, who are so driven by the idea of satisfying a kid's desire for the next best thing that they seem to forget why they're there. But no matter how people act, the pollsters report that nine and one half out of ten people said they believed in God.

In addition in 2005, 42 percent of all adults in America said they believed they had been visited by a ghost or departed spirit, usually a spouse or sibling. In 1994, in the same survey only 27 percent, still a high number, admitted that they believed they had been visited by a ghost of a departed loved one. But wait, the numbers get even better. In another 2005 survey, over two-thirds of all Americans said they had had some psychic or extra-sensory perception experience, a total almost 10 percent higher than a similar survey conducted twenty-two years ago.

Are psychic experiences on the rise or just the reports of such experiences? Are people more willing to talk about such experiences because the political or spiritual climate is more conducive to these kinds of conversations? I believe that both statements are true: psychic experiences are on the rise throughout the general population and people are more willing to talk about their experiences because, over the past quarter century, it's become okay to do so. This really is a quantum leap, especially in America where traditionally we have been very nervous about our supernatural beliefs and experiences.

Joel Martin in his forthcoming *The Haunting of America* reminds us that historically America has had a bifurcated view of spiritualism, New Age, and the paranormal. While our Puritan founders were eradicating anything that even smacked of supernatural, eradicating at the stake, I should say, presidents from George Washington through Ronald Reagan have willingly embraced the supernatural. Washington had a vision at Valley Forge, which predicted victory for the Colonies in the Revolutionary War. Washington reappeared to General McClellan to tell him to get off his butt and defend the capital. Washington appeared to the Maine regiment holding the hill, "Little Round Top," urging them to charge into the teeth of a

Confederate regiment, and Lincoln, Pierce, Wilson, Reagan, and Clinton all hosted seers, prognosticators, or mediums at the White House for advisory sessions or consultations. Yet, there are televangelists who argue that anyone who reports a UFO sighting or believes we should investigate UFOs is a sorcerer. The very same people argue that Shirley MacLaine is somehow un-American for advocating reincarnation and a spiritual lifestyle. In the face of this, therefore, it is heartening to see that an overwhelming majority of Americans not only believe in human spiritual experiences but almost half of us admit to having seen the departed spirits of loved ones.

Almost as if to reinforce the existence of what I want to call a multiverse reality, hard scientists—physicists and molecular biologists—are even further out on a limb than the Robert Monroes of the world. Scientists report discoveries that tend to show that what some might call hallucinations or flights of fancy are actually real. We have subsidiary brains in our stomachs; our cells have memories; time travel is theoretically possible and has been undertaken; reincarnation has a theoretical basis in fact; and human beings can physically influence the future. These are all recent discoveries or taken from reports of scientific experiments.

All this tells me that there is now a blurred line between supernatural and natural, paranormal and normal, alternate reality and reality. This is an extraordinary occurrence. But is there a deeper meaning to it? I say there is, as my show is into its final minutes and my call board is flashing with people wanting to report their own experiences. I suggest that humanity itself may be entering a new age, an age of a broader enlightenment, an age in which we discover that what we've believed to be an intangible spiritual potential is actually scientifically measurable. We're entering an age in which we actually implement the science to measure such things as were only ascertainable on faith. What a great age this will be. And you, my caller, are actually at the head of the wave.

Arthur C. Clarke described this age in his seminal science fiction novel, *Childhood's End*. Other writers have described what is happening to our species as the emergence of Indigo Children or Crystal Children. We've heard about this before in movies such as David Twyman's *Indigo*, in books such as *Jason* by Ann Andrews, and Neal David Walsh's *Conversations with God* and from authors like Lysette Larkin, and, now, from, of all places, *Pravda*. What is an Indigo Child? In a review of *Jason* in *UFO Magazine*, we define Indigo Children as kids who exhibit very strange and wonderful paranormal powers. We write that Indigos—so named because of the indigo aura around their bodies—have "the power to communicate telepathically . . . so as to form their own super-cybercommunications grid. Indigos can communicate with each other without speech and without even being in close proximity. Indigos have a purpose, however; a purpose that some of them don't even understand except that it is to help the planet and to help their human surrogate parents." We also say that "Indigos have an ability to rise out of the immediacy of past, present, and future and see the vast continuum of time in a single view."

According to a recent article in *Pravda*, an Indigo child's immune system is also more than a thousand times stronger than that of a regular person. Out-of-body experiences are almost commonplace for Indigos, who are able to project themselves across time and across galaxies, according to parents who have raised them. As the article in *Pravda* states, a young Latvian child is very casual about describing her astral travels to the ends of the universe. Her father is quick to deny his daughter's astral abilities in public. But in private he is not reluctant to use her higher sensory perception. The article quotes the girl's father as using her extraordinary level of awareness to guide him to the mechanical problems with his tractor. The father tells the *Pravda* reporter that his daughter "is always in the know what is wrong with the machine."

Although Indigo Children have been around for at least twenty years, having run into problems with the public school system and even with juvenile justice and criminal justice authorities well into the 1990s, their time is actually close at hand. Some, particularly author Ann Andrews, say that Indigo Children are part of a hybridized species—part human, part extraterrestrial—who represent the next stage of the intelligent design component of human evolution. These children, our progeny, will guide the way to ensuing generations of supernatural humans who have no qualms about implementing the very powers we have been talking about as part of their daily routine. You see, we are evolving, and you are the early adapters of a vast reservoir of human ability. But when will all this happen?

I've been saying for years that 2012, the Mayan calendar's end of time, will be the key date for human evolution. Will time stop? Will we be destroyed? Will we stand witness to the end of days? I don't think so. Here, again, *Pravda* suggests that 2012 has particular importance for Indigos. According to Mayan predictions, a great "transition" event will be taking place in 2012 "after the Sun and Earth form a straight line pointing to the center of the Galaxy." In effect, this line-up will create an entirely new dimensional paradigm in which human beings will be able to exist in a fourth dimension. However, this ability will only apply to those people who have already enhanced their understanding of reality—Indigo Children—so as to take advantage of the additional dimensional reality.

Will 2012 be a time of time travel? Paul H. Smith accomplished the feat of time travel all the way back in the 1980s, according to his book *Reading the Enemy's Mind* and his interview in *UFO Magazine*. I believe 2012 is a demarcation point into the fourth dimension into which human time travelers will go back to the dawn of human civilization. Those strange astronaut-like drawings Erich Von Daniken talks about in *Chariots of the Gods* and those strange airline runways across the Andes Mountains in Chile and Bolivia are not for extraterrestrial space craft. They're for us, human beings who return to the past and whose images are captured on the sides of rocks. We're the ones in the Renaissance painting space capsules and the helicopter hieroglyphs on the sides of the Egyptian pyramids.

A new age of evolved children is coming. *Pravda* says that an astounding 95 percent of children born after 1994 are Indigos. These are children with vastly more powerful immune systems than we have and a different structure of DNA. Thus, according to *Pravda,* potentially hundreds of inhabitants on this planet have already climbed to a new evolutionary stage. They are not humans, as we understand humans, but hybrids, blends of extraterrestrials and humans who will achieve the enlightenment bestowed upon them by their altered genetic structure. And we are already seeing the results of their impact on our own social structure.

However, because Indigos had so much trouble in the 1980s and 1990s, a new age of children has emerged called "Crystal Children." Perhaps, whoever or whatever is seeding our planet or whatever natural evolutionary forces are at work—you choose the reasoning behind this—in response to the difficulties Indigos encountered ten to fifteen years ago, a new, more resilient, group of children has emerged. Crystal Children, I'm told, have stronger telepathic and communicative powers, an almost uncanny ability to experience out-of-body travel, as if they're slipping through a seam in the space-time continuum, and the ability to live in a time slipstream. In this slipstream, they are literally out of time, standing aside while time rushes by them. No wonder their parents say they vibrate at a different frequency and seem to look through people into the entire timeline that stretches across a person's life. Wow!

Their natural powers, however, can be your acquired powers. And that's the beauty of intuition training, remote viewing training, out-of-body training, and the ultimate: time travel. You don't need the H. G. Wells time machine to journey into the future. Your intuition or your remote-viewing prowess can take you there. Astral project yourself into your own future and you will know the absolute serene confidence of being a member of the great link of all creation.

People ask me how I can deal with so many different types of people, how I can accommodate the needs of callers to *Coast to Coast*. Radio broadcasting is a high-stress business. So how can a person appear to be unstressed? Easier than it seems if you develop the abilities to meditate, let your intuitive signal flow, do your everyday exercises in future travel, and let your spirit soar out of your body into different times and places. You will be able, after some solid self-training, to walk down the halls of your office, popping by cubicle after cubicle, and know, absolutely know, what a person's thinking on the other side of that divider. And you will accomplish this not because you're spying, but because you're naturally in touch. You will know what I know, that we are all connected and all communicating.

All you have to do is turn on the internal speaker and you're on the network. It is a remarkable power that, fueled by love for your neighbor, will drive you to new limits of human potential.

You see, despite all the denials and the skeptics, despite the ravings of the debunkers and the moral scolds, the world I'm talking about is as real as the book in your hands. There is no difference between the so-called supernatural world and the three-dimensional world you're in. I bring you the great news that you, individually and collectively, have the higher-sensory perceptivity that my aunt Shafica discovered fifty years ago. Now it's up to you use it, to wield that power.

MY FAVORITE GHOST STORY

If you listen to Coast, *you'll know that I believe that ghosts and spirits are as real as the computer I'm writing on. Don't tell me there are no ghosts because I know there are. I believe in the immortality of the human spirit and no skeptic or debunker can convince me otherwise. Accordingly, I love stories about the immortality of the human spirit, ghost stories, stories of relatives who come back from the other side to help or counsel their loved ones. Here is one of my favorites.*

A man called my local show in St. Louis years ago and told me a story of how he was so depressed and nearly suicidal that he decided to take a big time out and drive. He drove for an hour out of the city coming upon a small lake and town. He needed to chill. He got out of the car and sat by the lake on a bench, watching ducks fly in and out, and just communing with the surroundings. An old man in coveralls came by and sat next to him and they chatted. He said he felt so good after the talk that he wasn't depressed any longer, talking to the old guy had made him feel so much better. He left and came back to the big city for a basic restart, that talk had done him so much good.

A year later, talk about results, he had a wife, a new career, and was on the top of his game, so he decided to go back and thank the old fellow. Arriving back in the town and not knowing the man's last name or where he lived, he went to the town's only barber and asked about the old gent. The barber instructed him to go to a white house at the top of the hill and talk to the man's daughter. My caller knew then something was wrong. He went to the house and knocked on the door. A woman answered and my caller said, "I came by to thank your father for his advice. He changed my life."

Just then the daughter stopped him and said, "You're the fifth person to come by over the years and thank me. But, you see, my father died fifteen years ago."

I'll never forget that story.

For tonight, as the first stirrings of children can be heard through the predawn darkness on the East Coast, here's one piece of advice. I tell my callers over the sound of bells jingling outside the studio, just figure out what makes you happy, go back to it, and do it. Do it with confidence, do it with ease, and do it with love.

As always, my lines are open.

INDEX